D0442698

PREVIOUS BOOKS BY GOD

The Last Testament: A Memoir by God

The Bible

The Quran

The Book of Mormon (ironically)

From the Mixed-Up Files of Mrs. Basil E. Frankweiler

THE BOOK OF ~~PSALMS~~ *PSLAMS*

97 Divine Diatribes on Humanity's Total Failure

by

GOD

with **Jesus** and **The Holy Ghost**

as dictated to
DAVID JAVERBAUM (@TheTweetOfGod)

Simon & Schuster

NEW YORK LONDON TORONTO SYDNEY NEW DELHI

Simon & Schuster
1230 Avenue of the Americas
New York, NY 10020

First Simon & Schuster hardcover edition December 2021

SIMON & SCHUSTER and colophon are registered trademarks
of Simon & Schuster, Inc.

For information about special discounts for bulk purchases,
please contact Simon & Schuster Special Sales at 1-866-506-1949
or business@simonandschuster.com.

The Simon & Schuster Speakers Bureau can bring authors to your
live event. For more information or to book an event, contact the
Simon & Schuster Speakers Bureau at 1-866-248-3049
or visit our website at www.simonspeakers.com.

Manufactured in the United States of America

10   9   8   7   6   5   4   3   2   1

Library of Congress Cataloging-in-Publication Data has been applied for.

ISBN 978-1-9821-7602-0
ISBN 978-1-9821-7604-4 (ebook)

To life on earth.

It was fun while it lasted.

Discontents

CHAPTER 3 CHURCH AND PSTATE

CHAPTER 4 PSEMANTICS

CHAPTER 5 PSPECIFICS

CHAPTER 6   HEALTH AND PSEXUALITY

CHAPTER 7   CONTEMPORARY PSOCIETY

CHAPTER 8 THE END

Foreword

NOTE: *Penis not to scale.*
Seriously. Ask around.

Three thousand years ago I set pen to papyrus to express my gratitude to God for helping me defeat Goliath, be crowned king of Judaea, restore the Ark of the Covenant to Jerusalem, and hook up with Bathsheba, which, *rowr.*

The Book of Psalms began as a group of 150 songs I composed over the course of my kingship and debuted at my monthly concert series, "Psalm-Enchanted Evenings." After my death their collected lyrics became one of the most popular books in the Bible, winning admirers among both Jews and Jew-haters alike. As it turned out, God was also a fan; so much so that now, over three millenia later, He, along with Jesus and the Holy Ghost ("My better two-thirds," as He modestly calls them), has decided to revise them. *Respond* to them, more accurately.

You see, the Lord Almighty et al. have appropriated my format, and are using it not to praise, as I did, but to belittle, admonish, and generally condemn *you*—not you personally, dear reader, but the entire money-grubbing, morality-ignoring, conspiracy-mongering, culture-canceling, Earth-killing human community.

And He asked me to write the foreword.

I agreed, of course; so He gave me the first draft, which as it happened would also be the final draft. (God likes to work quickly and move on, mistakes literally be damned.) He told me to read it, then write something that would prepare you for what you are about to experience.

Having devoured the entire draft in one increasingly horrified sitting, I can only say this:

In the Book of Psalms, I wrote, "The Lord is my shepherd."

In *The Book of Pslams,* that shepherd replies, "Go flock yourselves."

King David

CHAPTER 1

OPENING PSALVOS

PSLAM 1

Just the Worst

1 I curse humanity, and lament its creation, and loathe it to the depths of its miserable being; for it is the worst.

2 Just . . .

3 The . . .

4 Worst.

5 *Homo sapiens*, you are the worst, lowliest creature I ever made, and I made 350,000 different species of beetle; including five thousand that eat dung.

6 Of all male animals on Earth, human men are the worst; and of all females, human women; and of all nonbinaries, human nonbinaries; and of all babies, the human baby is easily the puniest, ugliest, and most wretched.

7 (I remember when I caused My own son to be "born" in a manger; to you he was a redeemer and a savior; to Me he was a shrieking toadstool slathered in chowder.)

8 Three thousand years ago, when the world wasn't the sweltering, microplasticked palm-oil plantation it is today, Grammy Award–winning lyrist King David wrote the Book of Psalms, 150 beautiful odes in My honor.

9 Now, with time running out on the human race in general— and the book-buying public in particular—and in light of

recent global developments that have turned history into a stand-up act too excruciating for Me not to heckle,

10 I, along with My better two-thirds, have written this response, *The Book of Pslams*, a furious jeremiad of doleful misanthropy published by the good people at Simon & Schuster.

11 In these pages you will find nearly a hundred versed vituperations in the form of psalvos (from Me), psermons (from Jesus), and psatires, pspoofs, and poetry pslams (from the Holy Ghost).

12 It's a book equally fit to serve as the basis of a new religion, or light reading on the shitter.

13 And, in much the same way that reading the Psalms always leaves Me feeling good about Myself, even by My own standards, it is My fondest hope that reading these Pslams will leave you feeling awful about yourselves, even by yours.

14 *Hey*, I can hear you thinking—because I'm omniscient and I can do that—*You sure talk a lot of crap about us, God, but didn't You make us in Your image? And if we're failures, doesn't that mean You're a failure? And if we're "the worst," doesn't that make You "the worst of the worst"?*

15 We'll get to that.

PSLAM 2
Come

"Come."
—Matthew 14:29

1 Hello. My name is Jesus Christ, and I am the Son of God.

2 I was born in Bethlehem in the year 4 or 5 BMe and died in Jerusalem thirty-three years later from what the coroner controversially ruled a "tragic accident."

3 Then three days later I rose from the dead, and, after mollifying local zombie hunters, joined my apostles in the ancient celebration of the vernal equinox, which they later pretended was a brand-new holiday called Easter.

4 Two thousand years have passed since then, time I've mostly spent dying for your sins, posing for portraits, appearing on breakfast foods, and trying to get my Dad not to torment you so often, so thoroughly, and with such boyish glee.

5 During this period a religion arose called Christianity, perhaps you've heard of it—oh you have, great—which, after a tenuous and martyr-tastic start, grew into a worldwide faith with more than 2.4 billion followers, the world's second-largest religious affiliation, after the Beyhive.

6 This religion even has its own bible, "The Bible," an account of my life and words as chronicled by four men with eerily common modern American names.

7 This account is incomplete; it's imperfectly translated; there's some duplication, some contradiction, and a few parables with *major* plot holes; but overall it gives a reasonably decent sense of my teachings.

8 And as the name implies, Christianity is based on those teachings.

9 Except it's not.

10 In practice, Christianity is based on my birth—miraculous, virginal, carol-worthy—and my death—degrading, gruesome, torture-porny—and has little to do with anything I said or did in the apparently inconsequential period between those two events known as "my life."

11 For many, including most of those who claim to be pious, Christianity is less a faith than a front, a feint, an excuse, a cover story, a private club, a get-out-of-hell-free card.

12 My philosophy and ethics are ignored at best and subverted at worst, and yet there's my name mocking me right in the name of the religion.

13 These days when I run into the Buddha and ask him how Buddhism is going and he says, "Great! Still kind of true to my teachings! What about Christianity?," I cringe and immediately change the subject to our mutual hatred of Jainism.

14 So when Dad told me He was writing this Book of Pslams, I saw an opportunity.

15 For while the original New Testament is hardly lacking for sermons, they seem to have failed to impact your moral outlook the way I hoped they would.

16 When I delivered them I was mindful to take my message of love and brotherhood and "dumb it down"; but looking at the world, it's clear you're in desperate need of a Second Dumbing.

17 Thus, Pops graciously provided me the literary real estate for a passel of new sermons, exegeses, and expository homilies, each of which will riff off one of my original, actual quotes from the Gospels.

18 This sermon is the first of those, and the one-word quote that starts it is what I told Peter as I walked on water; he didn't believe what he was seeing, so I said, "Come," invited him off his boat, and he too walked on water.

19 It was a wonderful moment, but let's be honest: that's not why I chose "Come" for my first chapter-and-verse header.

20 I'm two millennia older and wiser now, and I know my audience better.

21 And you're all a bunch of pervs.

The Holy Ghostwriter

1 I am the Holy Ghostwriter, a third of the divinity,

2 The shyest and most esoteric member of the Trinity,

3 A self-effacing Godhead, although one with an affinity

4 For entering a woman's ear and taking her virginity.

5 The Father, Son, and I have lived for ages immemorial,

6 As three, but also one; math mystic and phantasmagorial.

7 But since we're consubstantial, we are never territorial,

8 And that is why the book you hold is triply co-authorial.

9 My portions will be passages of poetry and parody.

10 They're heavy on the irony, but light on the vulgarity,

11 With many satirizing works of great familiarity.

12 (The sources of these spoofs will be identified for clarity.)

13 So please enjoy my humble bids at verbal ingenuity.

14 Their contrast with the other Pslams may seem an
    incongruity.

15 I wasn't sure my work was any good, but looking through it, e—

16 Ven Jesus told me, "Holy Ghost, this format suits you to a T!"

Only One

1 Of the millions of varieties of living things that populate the wondrous planet I have bequeathed unto you, only one has the ability to buy this book.

2 It is not only the same one that created an enormous global electronic retail and distribution system to ensure you receive it by tomorrow,

3 But the same one with the audacity to name that system for the enormous rain forest whose destruction your order will accelerate.

4 Numerous are the beasts of the field who travel long, grueling miles across the earth in search of food;

5 But only one who travels long, grueling miles *without going anywhere*, in search of a "Lookin' fierce, TwinsMom42!" from the Peloton instructor.

6 All creatures require water to survive; but only one, upon achieving fame, demands *bottled* water, and orders his or her tour manager to put that in the contract rider.

7 Countless are the female animals who suckle their young; yet only one writes think pieces about her "conflicting wave of emotions" while doing it in a restaurant.

8 And countless are the male animals who hasten away upon mating; yet only one reunites with his child six years later following a DNA test on *The Maury Show.*

9 All animals excrete waste, but only one freshens the air surrounding its newly deposited feces so as to foster the illusion that it poops pine cones.

10 Every living being consumes other living beings, but only one kills for reasons other than survival; sport, art, commerce, and a hundred other nonessential motives drive it to slaughter all manner of animals, and plants, and even fungi;

11 Which are not plants, but their own separate taxonomic kingdom; a lot of people don't know that.

12 All organisms are the end result of billions of years of evolution, but only one has the intelligence to discover it.

13 Or the stubbornness to deny it.

14 All living things reproduce, but only one can consciously limit its ability to do so.

15 The same one that *should*.

16 Finally, of the millions of species living on this planet, only one knows he's going to die.

17 The same one that, out of spite, is taking all the others with him.

PSLAM 5

The Thrill

1 Humanity, there are many times I look back on Day Six of creation and wish I'd stopped before I made you.

2 Then, since I was working alphabetically, the last animal I created would have been the zebu, which would be a much happier memory; I love the zebu; it's a thinking man's ox.

3 And yet I will be honest: the thrill isn't entirely gone.

4 There are still things about you I adore, things that take Me back to a simpler, happier time, when life was young and love was new and produce regulations were still respected.

5 Your body still amazes Me; it's incredible; I get excited every time I see one.

6 Your mind too; I'm still in awe of it; not always what it does, but what it conceives, *how* it conceives; it's the most gorgeously complex thing in the universe.

7 I still love the way you whisper when we're alone, falling to your knees, entrusting Me with your deepest secrets and desires, and telling Me I'm the only one.

8 I could never find your restless curiosity anything but endearing.

9 I could never find your urge to create the new and beautiful old and ugly.

10 And your laugh . . . never in a trillion years could I grow tired of hearing you laugh.

11 I love how under the right circumstances you will drop everything and risk your own lives to help a loved one, a stranger, a community, a world; I only wish you'd find more right circumstances.

12 And I hate to admit it, but I guess I'm still in love with the whole human "thing."

13 Birth, childhood, adolescence, youth, adulthood, middle age, old age, death, war, peace, love, hate, weekdays, weekends, wins, losses, business, pleasure, friendship, rivalry, sex, marriage, parenthood, divorce, happiness, sadness, disappointment, satisfaction, food, booze, drugs, poverty, riches, health, sickness, adventure, tedium, despair, ecstasy, grief, joy, the whole dizzying, maddening, intoxicating, terrifying, stupefying, inexplicable experience.

14 I still dig it.

15 No, the thrill isn't gone, humanity; when I see you I still feel the same giddy rush of excitement I felt watching Adam and Eve frolic in the garden.

16 But honestly, in the long term . . .

17 I just don't see a future with you in it.

Love Your Enemies

*"But I tell you, love your enemies, and
pray for those who persecute you."*
—Matthew 5:44

1 I stand by those words; they are beautiful; they are empathetic; they are the cornerstone of any kind, humane society.

2 But they were also uttered before 2016.

3 I know many of you these days are finding it hard to love or pray for *anything,* much less your enemies and persecutors.

4 (Indeed, from the mouth of a Christian, the very phrase "I'll pray for you" more or less means "Go to hell.")

5 So if loving your enemies proves too difficult, try finding common ground with them, so you can at least recognize you're both members of the same species.

6 Think of it the way a good host might introduce two of her guests at a bipartisan cocktail party.

7 "You're carbon-based, right? I believe Donald here is carbon-based too!"

8 "How funny: you and Senator Cruz are from the same hemisphere!"

9 "What are the odds you and Tucker Carlson would *both* be wearing *shoes* to the party!"

10 As for praying for those who persecute you . . . that's an even taller order.

11 During my ministry on Earth I had a few vicious persecutors for whom I found it very difficult to pray.

12 Sometimes I'd trick myself by mentally superimposing a more morally attractive person's face on his, then imagining I was praying for *him*.

13 (Once, I was praying for Judas Iscariot, and right as I finished I screamed, "John the Baptist! I love you, John!"

14 Awkward.)

15 *Genuinely* loving your enemies and *sincerely* praying for those who persecute you is an achievement reserved for only a small handful of saints; and we all know what usually happens to saints:

16 They die at the hands of the enemies they loved and the persecutors they prayed for.

17 So by way of throwing you a moral bone, I hereby modify my biblical injunction for modern usage.

18 *Love your enemies to the extent possible, and pray for those who persecute you not to suffer more than necessary.*

19 There.

20 Difficult, but doable.

PSLAM 7

Christ's in the Cradle

Written in the voice of the Father, about the Son, by the Holy Ghost.

1 My child arrived just the other day.

2 He came to the world an unusual way.

3 But there were lives to guide and fates to sway.

4 I sent a card every Christmas Day.

5 And he was talkin' 'fore I knew it, and as he grew,

6 He'd say, "I'm coeternal with You, Dad. You know I'm coeternal with You."

7 And the Christ's in the Cradle and the word's made flesh.

8 Mary in blue and the ass in the crèche.

9 "When You comin' down, Dad?" "I don't know when,

10 But we'll get together then, son. You know we'll have the end times then."

11 My child healed men just the other day.

12 He said, "This is a ball, Dad! Come on, let's pray!

13 Will You speak to my flock?" I said, "Not today.

14 I got a king to smite." He said, "That's OK."

15 He walked away, but he looked right at Me.

16 He said, "I'm gonna be like Thee, Dad. You know I'm gonna be like Thee."

17 *(Repeat verses 7–10.)*

18 Well, he came from Supper just the other day.

19 Too much like a man; still, I thought I'd say,

20 "Son, I'm proud of you, join Me up in the sky."

21 He grabbed his wrists, and he said with a sigh,

22 "What I'd really like, Dad, is to die on the cross now.

23 Three days later send me back, somehow."

24 *(Repeat verses 7–10.)*

25 I've long stopped trying; My son never did.

26 The other day I appeared to the kid.

27 I said, "I'd like to have you here by my side."

28 He said, "I'd love to, Dad, but I've been crucified.

29 You see, I'm busy with the dyin' and redeemin' I do.

30 But it's sure nice talkin' to You, Dad. It's sure nice talkin' to You."

31 And as I sat on the throne, it occurred to Me: My boy was not like Me, no.

32 My boy . . . was *not* like Me.

33 *(Repeat verses 7–10.)*

PSLAM 8

Forsaken

1 "My God, my God, why hast Thou forsaken me?"

2 That's the first line of Psalm 22 in the Old Testament, which Jesus quoted on the cross in the New Testament, making it the only major biblical quote to appear in both books (although see Pslam 91 for a clarification).

3 It's clearly one of your biggest theological FAQs, and I'm happy to answer it . . . by asking *you* a few questions.

4 Why *shouldn't* I forsake you?

5 If you were Me, wouldn't *you* forsake you?

6 Given where you are right now as a species, society, and planet, and given My unlimited access to, you know, *the universe*, how much more time and effort and attention would *you* put into Project *Homo sapiens* before screaming "SCREW IT!" and starting all over again on one of those sexy young rocks orbiting Betelgeuse?

7 Ever thought to ask yourselves, "Why have we forsaken nature?" or "Why have we forsaken one another?" or "Why have I forsaken myself?"

8 Any of those queries ever pop into those needy little frontal lobes of yours?

9 Also, how do you think "Why hast Thou forsaken me?" makes you sound?

10 Don't you think that every time I hear it I send an arch-angel to fetch heaven's smallest violin so I can play it sar-castically to the comedic delight of the floating-room-only cherubim crowd?

11 And finally: *Did you ever think that maybe constantly hear-ing you moan variations on "Why hast Thou forsaken me?" is a big reason why I've forsaken thee?*

12 Mankind up, people.

13 You're still not nearly as God-forsaken as Earth is man-forsaken.

PSLAM 9
WWID?

"I am the way, the truth, and the life: no man cometh unto the Father, but by me."
—John 14:6

1 People always ask, "What would Jesus do?"

2 (They even wear "What Would Jesus Do?" bracelets; in that case, "what I would do" is immediately take off those bracelets, because not only are they ugly, the wrist is the *last* place on my body that needs further accessorizing.)

3 I understand the thinking behind the question: I'm a paragon of virtue, so if everyone behaved as I did in the Bible, the world would be a better place.

4 The problem is, what I would do then is very different from what I would do now.

5 *Then*, if you asked what I would do, I would preach love and kindness and patience and forbearance and forgiveness.

6 *Now*, if you asked what I would do, I would respond like so:

7 ¯_(ツ)_/¯

8 Note that this is not the shrug emoji, but the shrug *emoticon*, which, while more old-fashioned, has a wry fatalism that 🙏 lacks; and wry fatalism is *precisely* the attitude I wish to convey.

9 "Jesus, we don't know whether to kill one another or not. What would *you* do?"

10 ¯_(ツ)_/¯

11 "Jesus, we don't know whether to save our planet or destroy it. What would *you* do?"

12 ¯_(ツ)_/¯

13 "Jesus, we don't know whether it's right or wrong to perform forced hysterectomies on detained immigrant women. What would *you* do?"

14 ಠ_ಠ   ¯_(ツ)_/¯   ಠ_ಠ

15 It's not that these are rhetorical questions. They're not.

16 They have answers, and you can probably guess what they are.

17 But I've already answered them, explicitly or implicitly, for anyone who truly *wants* them answered; and while I love you and enjoy dying for you as much as ever, at a certain point, when you've provided enough direction and shed enough blood and made the general humanistic tenor of your philosophy sufficiently apparent, and yet it still keeps getting mocked and undermined on scales great and small at a pace that will lead to accelerating calamity on the global level and accelerating unhappiness on the personal, all you can do, or want to do, when asked yet again to serve as an ethical straw man on some issue you know your opinion of which will in the end be reverently ignored, is

18 ¯_(ツ)_/¯

19 So *that's* what I would do.

20 In fact I'm going to do it right now, while I work.

21 | ‾ |
22   [===¯_(ツ)_/¯===]
23 | |
24 | |
25 | |
26 |_|

Die! Decline!

Based on the summer-camp favorite "Rise and Shine (The Noah Song)."

1 The Lord said to humans, "You're gonna cause a floody, floody!"

2 God said to humans, "You're gonna cause a floody, floody!

3 Does that bother (clap!) anybody, -body?"

4 Children of the Lord!

5 So die! Decline! Your end will be gory, gory!

6 Die! Decline! Your end will be gory, gory!

7 Die! Decline! Your (clap!) end will be gory, gory,

8 Children of the Lord!

9 The citizens, were kept in, were kept in the darky, darky.

10 Citizens, were kept in, were kept in the darky, darky

11 By the rich white (clap!) patriarchy, -archy,

12 Children of the Lord!

13 The temperature, it went up by tenths of degreesies, -eesies.

14 Temperature, it went up by tenths of degreesies, -eesies.

15 Brought the planet (clap!) to its kneesie-weesies,

16 Children of the Lord!

17 The oceans, they went up, they went up by inchy-inchy.

18 Oceans, they went up, they went up by inchy-inchy.

19 Mass extinction (clap!) was a cinchy, cinchy,

20 Children of the Lord!

21 The sun came out and heated the landy, landy.

22 Sun came out and heated the landy, landy.

23 Turned the green parts (clap!) brown and sandy-wandy,

24 Children of the Lord!

25 Now that is the end of, the end of the story, story.

26 That is the end of, the end of the story, story.

27 Take it as your (clap!) memento mori, mori,

28 Children of the Lord!

29 So die! Decline! Your end will be gory, gory!

30 Die! Decline! Your end will be gory, gory!

31 Die! Decline! Your (clap!) end will be gory, gory,

32 Children of the Lord!

North Sentinel Island

1 Have you heard of North Sentinel Island?

2 It's a small speck in the Indian Ocean that's home to the Sentinelese, an uncontacted tribe that has lived in total isolation since the Stone Age.

3 Outsiders trying to make contact with the Sentinelese often meet a gruesome and painful end.

4 But once you get to know them, they're some of the nicest folks you'd ever want to meet.

5 I like to swing by NSI about once a week and pass a pleasant hour or two with the people; so as not to compromise their paganism I speak from the large rock they've long regarded as their chief god; rightly so, it now turns out.

6 Sometimes I put the heavenly reverb on and lay a small "thou shalt" guilt trip on them, but mostly we just sit around and chitchat.

7 We'll talk about coral, and the new coconuts, and that big stingray they just caught; and I'll get the latest gossip, and catch up with the Klkmúav!kti family, and check in on little Tʰikʰwa-gopejajo; his foreskin was just axed off; it looks *adorable*.

8 I visit the Sentinelese precisely because they are primitive: unspoiled, uncorrupted by civilization, among the last

people on Earth completely attuned to the here and now, to the miracle of My creation.

9 They don't ask for anything, they don't complain about anything, and they don't seek forgiveness for anything, because they lack the self-awareness to call anything evil or good.

10 It's like they never Fell.

11 On November 17, 2018, I was visiting NSI when I became aware that a Christian missionary, John Allen Chau, was about to be dropped off on the island alone for the third time.

12 (By the way, "become aware" is the closest I can get to describing My epistemology.

13 Omniscience doesn't so much mean that I *know* everything, but that I *can* if I want to; and I usually don't.

14 I find that complete knowledge of the past, present, and future gets a little predictable; so with some exceptions I dole out information to Myself only on a need-to-know-everything basis.)

15 The previous day Chau had kayaked to the shore and left gifts, but paddled off when the tribe began stringing their bows at him.

16 Then he returned and tried to speak with them, only to swim away in terror when they seized his boat and little Tʰikʰwa-gopejajo shot an arrow right through his waterproof Bible.

17 Now, in perfect accordance with the comedy rule of threes, he was approaching once more, and since the tribespeople

had gathered from his self-righteous demeanor that he had some evangelistic purpose in mind, they asked My opinion as to what they should do with him.

18 And I thought of the thousands of other islands where missionaries had come over the centuries.

19 And I thought of the millions of other natives living simple, happy lives who had never known they were horrible hellbound sinners until someone was loving enough to travel halfway around the world just to tell them.

20 And I thought of the net result of the efforts to spread the Gospel in the Americas, and Africa, and the Pacific, even the well-intentioned ones; what it had done to lives, and cultures, and languages, and lands, and nations, and human history, and, above all, to My reputation as a beneficent, peaceful deity.

21 And I gave them My opinion.

22 And he was delicious.

CHAPTER 2

PSPIRITUALITY

Born Again

"Except a man be born again, he cannot see the kingdom of God."

—John 3:3

1 *Again.*

2 Not *yesterday.*

PSLAM 13

John 3:16

"For God so loved the world, that He gave His only begotten Son, that whosoever believeth in him should not perish but have everlasting life."
—John 3:16

1 What a deal!

2 John, are you *really* telling the good folks reading this at home that they can live forever in paradise for the low, low price of believing in just *one* Son of God (me)?

3 Amazing! It sounds too good to be true! But then again, so do I, ha ha!

4 And there's no catch?

5 So you're saying those millions of previously blissful tribes-people who converted to Christianity—some voluntarily, some in ignorance, some by force—all got everlasting life?

6 They *did*?! Wow! Great work, missionaries! I guess all that disease you spread was a smallpox to pay!

7 And the babies who died before they were old enough to accept me as their Lord and Savior, or even be baptized? *They* got everlasting life?

8 What's that you say? "The Bible never explicitly says that's the case, but sure, let's go with that"?

9 Well, that's a comforting enough answer for me, or any grieving parent!

10 Oooh, here's a tough one: What about a nonbeliever who has a deathbed conversion?

11 It counts?!

12 But what if the person is bad?

13 Like, *really* bad?

14 Someone who's lived a life of crime, immorality, deceit, treachery, mayhem, discord, violence, cruelty, hypocrisy, harm, and hatred?

15 A life spent damaging, ruining, or even killing other people?

16 The kind of life where all those gathered around his deathbed (if anyone's even there) know the world was worse for his being in it and will be better once he's gone?

17 That still counts?!

18 OK, then I have to ask: What if this same awful person didn't even *need* a deathbed conversion because he'd believed in me—or at least claimed to, loudly and publicly and completely hypocritically—his whole awful life?

19 *That still counts?!*

20 Amazing.

21 Well, if *this* isn't an offer guaranteed to produce a decent society, I don't know *what* is!

22 So don't delay, heathens: Cash in on this amazing opportunity to ensure yourself eternal life by believing in me today. Act now!

23 *Offer not valid in Florida.*

24 *Terms and fine points of sectarian doctrine may apply.*

25 *No idiot holding a "John 3:16" poster at a sporting event will be eligible for this promotion.*

PSLAM 14
Prayer 101

1 No force on Earth is stronger than prayer.

2 They say prayer can move mountains, but it can do far more: it can raise valleys; straighten fjords; lengthen isthmuses; even unite all the islands in an archipelago into one island, thereby eliminating the need for inter-island ferry service.

3 Yes, *nothing* is more powerful than prayer, either in geography or in life.

4 And as the Lord thy God, *nothing* is more important to Me than providing each and every customer with quick, reliable prayer-answering service.

5 But prayer is a two-way street.

6 It only works if you do it right.

7 And most people do *not* do it right.

8 The vast majority of prayers go unanswered simply because the vast majority of the people offering them don't know what the hell they're doing.

9 Trust Me, if you were in My position, you would lose your *mind* watching all the amateur-hour supplicatory mistakes people make.

10 Mistakes in posture, elocution, facial expression, eye movement, specificity, scheduling, focus, depth of faith, clarity

of purpose, inner spiritual alignment with the divine Will, grammar . . . you name it.

11 Even the fundamentals, like finger positioning.

12 Do you know how many people I see every day praying with their hands clasped but their pinkies aligned at different heights?

13 7,498,023, on average, that's how many.

14 Listen: when someone prays correctly, I answer the prayer *on* time, *every* time.

15 That's the God Guarantee.®

16 But I refuse to feel guilty when a believer asks for a favor using sloppy technique and then gets mad at Me when, I don't know, his dog dies.

17 That's not a Me problem, that's a *thee* problem.

18 If you want your prayers answered, all you have to do is pray correctly.

19 Correctly, and for things that were going to happen anyway.

Requests

1 Each day the vast celestial switchboards jam

2 With calls for whom or what God ought to "bless,"

3 Or with the righteous ringing to express

4 Their views on what or whom He ought to "damn,"

5 Or whose new risky journey He should "speed,"

6 Or which events "forbid," or sins "forgive,"

7 Or queens "save" (not "save," really; more "let live"):

8 A billion brusque imperatives of need.

9 But God is *God*, and not the mighty slave

10 Or friendly flunky your demands presume;

11 And your words *never* alter what or whom

12 He'll bless, damn, speed, forbid, forgive, or save.

13 God is the haughty host of fussy guests

14 Who rudely make what He won't take: requests.

Treasure in Heaven

"Sell all thou hast, and distribute it unto the poor,
and thou shalt have treasure in heaven."
—Luke 18:22

1 So how's that going?

2 The selling all thou hast and distributing it unto the poor, I mean.

3 You guys finished yet?

4 'Cause I know there's a lot of logistics involved, a lot of inter-generational torch-passing and such, but it's been, what, two millennia? Something like that?

5 I don't mean to nudge, it's just that Luke 18:22 isn't the only place in the Gospels where I *specifically, explicitly* enjoin my followers to sell all their possessions.

6 There's also Luke 12:33 and Matthew 19:21.

7 If you read the Bible regularly, as I know so many of you Christians do—because you *say* you do—you can't miss it.

8 Boy, I'll tell you, the poor are really going to appreciate the wealth redistribution; the *socialism*, to put it more succinctly; I'm sure you're all comfortable with that term, "socialism," since that's the philosophy I espouse, as any objective reader of the Bible can see.

9 It's not that I question the good intentions of prominent fundamentalists—televangelists, for example.

10 Televangelists are good people.

11 Good, *good* people.

12 And I know they fly on private jets only to get a better view of the impoverished millions around the globe to whom they're *thisclose* to giving all their money.

13 Anyway, let me know when the last of the wealthy is done selling all he or she hath.

14 Again, sorry for nagging.

15 It's just that when pastors preach that you're their Savior, and raise money in your name, yet not only ignore a clear mandate you've given in three separate passages of the Holy Book they claim to live by, but fleece their followers and then hoard their riches . . .

16 Well, it's just something you notice.

17 Assholes.

Joel Osteen

1 28 US Code §4101 defines "defamation" as "any proceeding for libel, slander, or similar claim alleging that forms of speech are false, have caused damage to reputation or emotional distress . . . or have resulted in criticism, dishonor, or condemnation of any person."

2 At first glance this may seem like a broad definition, but in fact it makes pursuing a successful defamation lawsuit quite difficult.

3 If a negative public statement cannot be shown to be *objectively* incorrect, judges will not deem that allegation "defamatory" or "false."

4 Therefore, the statement that Joel Osteen looks like the love child of Tim Allen and Martin Short whom they lacquered, Botoxed, fitted with a cryogenically frozen smile, and dropped in the Liberty University trash bin is not "false."

5 The same standards apply to attacks on a public figure's character.

6 For example, one prominent social critic recently drew fire for describing Osteen's so-called prosperity gospel as "a horrific desecration of every single principle espoused in the New Testament."

7 Harsh words; but here again an ideological *interpretation* cannot legally be considered "false," indemnifying the

aforementioned Osteen-hater, who in this case happened to be My son Jesus Christ.

8 An offended party only has grounds for action when the allegation in question can be *definitively* disproven.

9 During 2017's Hurricane Harvey, for instance, several major print publications accused Joel Osteen of shutting the doors of his church to those displaced by the storm.

10 Had those accusations been in any way false, Osteen would have been well within his rights to seek restitution for defamation of character.

11 They weren't, though.

12 He shut his doors to storm victims.

13 Until he was finally shamed into offering shelter.

14 That's what he did.

15 He did that.

16 So to conclude, an author cannot be found guilty of libel or slander for an observation that is not factually disprovable.

17 Such as, "Joel Osteen is a greedy hypocrite."

18 Or "Joel Osteen is an unctuous charlatan."

19 Or "Joel Osteen once said, 'Do not swallow anything Satan is trying to ram down your throat. Jesus comes first.'"

20 Seriously, google it. Guy's a moron.

PSLAM 18
The Hate Prayer of Franklin Graham

"You will be hated by all for my name's sake."
—Matthew 10:22

1 Man, make me an instrument of your hate.

2 Where there is peace, let me sow strife;

3 Where there is broad-mindedness, dogma;

4 Where there is tolerance, bigotry;

5 Where there is rationality, hysteria;

6 Where there is unity, division;

7 Where there are humans, heathens.

8 O pious hypocrites, use me, Jesus, not so much to seek

9 To promote brotherhood as to prevent it,

10 To urge humility as to mock it,

11 To end war as to justify it.

12 For it is in demonizing that you feel angelic,

13 It is in moralizing that you feel moral,

14 And it is in killing in my name that you feel most alive.

PSLAM 19

The Timidity Prayer

From Apostolics Anonymous.

1 God, grant me the timidity to absolve You for the prayers that aren't answered,

2 The sycophancy to thank You for the prayers that are,

3 And the discretion not to notice the difference.

Monopolytheism

1 Zeus has gone and Ra's moved on and Odin's long departed.

2 Indra's day has slipped away, and Marduk's barely started.

3 Pantheons of stone and bronze have passed from human prodding:

4 Against all odds, amongst all gods, God is the last one godding.

5 Those other lords had helpful hordes of lesser lights to rule with,

6 But He has none, except His son, whom anyone can fool with.

7 The cosmic throne is His alone; He would not choose to share it.

8 And yet of late the world's sad fate has made it hard to bear it.

9 Your use of His creation is so callous and abusive,

10 The evidence of your offense so palpably conclusive,

11 The sorrow that He suffers at your current state so crippling,

12 That from the walls of heaven's halls a rumor's started rippling

13 That gods of old may soon be told to ready for their sequels,

14 To thunder back to pick up slack, as aides if not as equals,

15 A sacred crew to help Him through the coming cataclysm.

16 To share the pain, God may ordain monopoly theism.

PSLAM 21
Clickbait

"Let no man deceive you with empty words, for because of such words God's wrath falls on those who are disobedient."
—Ephesians 5:6

1 <u>She Was a Virgin. She Got Pregnant. She's *Still* a Virgin.</u>

2 <u>Turn Your Manger into a Delivery Room: Here's How!</u>

3 <u>Three Gifts Your Newborn Savior Will Love *(#3 Will Shock You!)*</u>

4 <u>They Laughed When He Called Himself the Son of God. Then He Started Preaching.</u>

5 <u>They Had Water. They Needed Wine. You Won't *Believe* What Happened Next.</u>

6 <u>You're Removing the Mote from Your Brother's Eye All Wrong</u>

7 <u>He Was Robbed and Left for Dead. Then a Samaritan Walked By.</u>

8 <u>Expert Reveals Surprising Strategy for Cheek Attack</u>

9 <u>5,000 People. Five Loaves. Two Fishes. You Won't *Believe* What Happened Next.</u>

10 <u>11 Apostles You Need to Be Following Right Now . . . and One to Avoid</u>

11 <u>The LAST Supper Recipe You'll Ever Need</u>

PSLAM 22

The Quran

1 The Quran reads like the posthumous flash-drive manifesto of a loner who shot up his gym class.

2 Sorry; it does.

3 It's "nonbelievers" this and "enemies" that, and "harsh anger" this and "fierce wrath" that, and "severe punishment" this and "the severest *possible* punishment" that, and more than half its 114 *surahs* discuss or at least refer to Judgment Day, although for some reason not one of them talk about Judgment *Night*, which I promise you will be a lot more fun, and catered.

4 "Slow down there, sultan," you say. "Didn't *You* write the Quran and send the archangel Gabriel to dictate it to Muhammad between 609 and 632 AD?"

5 No. Gabriel went rogue.

6 Long story-of-the-founding-of-a-religion short: at the time, Gabriel was mad at Me for denying him a promotion from archangel to *arch*-archangel.

7 He was bitter about it and chose to spend the next twenty-three years getting back at Me by whispering, in an Arab merchant's ear, a combination of sublimated revenge fantasies and sarcastic words of praise that, as you now all know, don't seem so sarcastic on paper.

8 So I can see how the Quran might incite some impressionable readers to jihad, just as the Buddhist sutras might incite some impressionable readers to the far stupider and more dangerous practice of meditation.

9 Having said all this, let Me be clear: I am *not* Islamophobic.

10 There are 1.8 billion Muslims in the world, most of them great people; I have tremendous respect for their rich culture, and when it comes to worshipping Me *no one* prays harder or more obsessively.

11 I mean, laying out a carefully tended prayer rug pointed towards Mecca and performing ritualized calisthenics in My honor *five times a day*?

12 It's *very* flattering.

13 Also I have great admiration for My prophet Muhammad, who was and remains the nicest guy you'd ever want to marry your nine-year-old daughter to.

14 All I'm saying is that the book he dictated is a little scary.

15 And sometimes keeps Me up at night.

Dayenu!

Based on everyone's favorite seder singalong.

1 If God brought you out of Egypt,

2 But then did not give you the land of Israel,

3 *Dayenu!*

4 If God gave you the land of Israel,

5 But then didn't let the Babylonians deport you,

6 *Dayenu!*

7 If God did let the Babylonians deport you,

8 But then didn't frame you for all time as "Christ killers,"

9 *Dayenu!*

10 If God did frame you for all time as "Christ killers,"

11 But then protected you so medieval society wasn't more or less the thousand-year story of large groups of Jews being scapegoated and persecuted,

12 *Dayenu!*

13 If God didn't protect you so medieval society wasn't more or less the thousand-year story of large groups of Jews being scapegoated and persecuted,

14 But then quashed the Inquisition, which despite Mel Brooks's best efforts was not all that funny,

15 *Dayenu!*

16 If God didn't quash the Inquisition, which despite Mel Brooks's best efforts was not all that funny,

17 But then did prevent pogroms from becoming Russia's favorite spectator sport for three hundred years running,

18 *Dayenu!*

19 If God didn't prevent pogroms from becoming Russia's favorite spectator sport for three hundred years running,

20 But then stopped a little something called the Holocaust, maybe you've heard of it, big incident, quite a few casualties,

21 *Dayenu!*

22 If God didn't stop a little something called the Holocaust, maybe you've heard of it, big incident, quite a few casualties,

23 But then did permit Israelis to have a single day go by without some of them being killed and/or killing others,

24 *Dayenu!*

25 If God didn't permit Israelis to have a single day go by without some of them being killed and/or killing others,

26 But then did keep *shanda* for the goyim like Bernie Madoff and Jeffrey Epstein and Harvey Weinstein and Alan Dershowitz out of the news,

27 *Dayenu!*

28 If God didn't keep *shanda* for the goyim like Bernie Madoff and Jeffrey Epstein and Harvey Weinstein and Alan Dershowitz out of the news,

29 But then did keep His allegedly "Chosen People" from suffering through a history that could have easily allowed me to make this song twenty times longer,

30 *Dayenu!*

The Monsignor

1 There was a monsignor named Guido

2 Who lived by the Catholic credo

3 Of tending his sheep

4 With a love wise and deep

5 While tending his lambs like a pedo.

6 "Now don't blow this out of proportion,"

7 He'd tell them by way of extortion.

8 "What I want from you

9 Is the least you can do

10 For saving you from an abortion."

Saintliness

1 There are over ten thousand saints recognized by the Catholic Church, most too obscure to loan their names to cities, universities, or Caribbean islands.

2 A few snuck in under the ethical radar, achieving canonization via corruption or politics or, in one sordid case, the deceased's sister paying a late-night visit to the pope and "cleansing his taint of sin."

3 But the majority of saints really were men and women of virtue and sanctity who devoted and sometimes gave their lives to the service of others.

4 St. Nicholas, for example, dedicated his days to bestowing presents upon nice children.

5 St. Patrick spent his life organizing green and boozy parades.

6 And St. Bernard disappeared heroically trying to deliver whiskey to lost hikers in the Alps.

7 True sainthood is a form of genius, and you could no more hope to accomplish what Martin Luther King Jr. did than you could Mozart or Einstein.

8 King and the small group of people like him were born with the capacity to live and function in the rarefied ultraviolet range of the moral spectrum, their vision illuminated by a radiant light others can neither perceive nor long tolerate without being consumed in its purity.

9 Conversely, another small group of people, like Stalin, Pol Pot, and the forty-fifth president of the United States, are innately comfortable in the infrared range of the spectrum, using this ability to confidently lead unseeing masses into terrifying darkness.

10 And somewhere in between, in the B-list region of visible light, reside the regular flawed human beings like you.

11 No amount of yoga retreats will make you ultraviolet, and no amount of hedge-fund trading will make you infrared.

12 But over the course of your life, it is possible, and indeed a considerable achievement, to move at least one or two moral Pantones closer to sainthood.

13 So in this world, let your modest goal be the advancement of your spiritual state from, say, azure to cobalt.

14 Then cerulean.

15 Then who knows? Maybe even teal.

16 The point is, try your best to end up in a blue state.

Evolution vs. Creationism

1 Evolution is wrong.

2 Trust Me.

3 I created the entire universe in six days—ironically, nearly *exactly* the amount of time it would take to binge-watch every episode of *The Big Bang Theory.*

4 So to all the "rationalists" out there with their "theories" and "evidence" and "literally millions of pieces of inarguable proof," let Me ask a few questions:

5 If evolution is real, why are supposedly Jurassic Age dinosaur bones always found at the same geological stratum as the *modern*-age humans who are finding them?

6 If evolution is real, why is there a wooded area on the top of Mount Ararat that you can take a satellite photo of and squint at and convince yourself is shaped like an ark?

7 If evolution is real, why is there a book that says it isn't? *How is that even possible?*

8 If evolution is real, why have the thousands of certified instances of carbon dating never led to *a single case* of carbon marriage?

9 If evolution is real, then aren't you descended from apes? Isn't that disgusting?

10 Isn't it much nicer to believe you're the descendant of one couple and their incestuous children and grandchildren?

11 If evolution is real, why does "creation science" have "science" in its name, yet "evolution" doesn't? Which sounds more "scientific" to you?

12 If evolution is real, why are you wrong because I said so and you're stupid and shut up?

13 And, if somehow all these arguments still leave you unconvinced, I'll end with the most powerful of all:

14 If evolution is real, why is the species that is supposedly its climax, the most evolved and advanced creature of them all, quite obviously the one *least well adapted* to live symbiotically with other species, preserve its environment, and give itself the best chance at long-term survival?

15 Would Mother Nature really be so cruel?

16 No.

17 *But would I?*

18 Hope you have an ice pack handy, Charles Darwin, 'cause you just got *burned*.

PSLAM 27

Raca

"Whosoever is angry with his brother without a cause shall be in danger of the judgment: and whosoever shall say to his brother, 'Raca,' shall be in danger of the council."
—Matthew 5:22

1 *"What the hell is 'Raca'?"*

2 A fair question, hypothetical mildly angry reader.

3 "Raca" is a Latin insult that some translate to "empty head," others "a worthless person," and still others "fool."

4 But the truth is, in the Galilean slanguage of the first century AD, "raca" meant "douchebag."

5 Look: this was my Sermon on the Mount, my big ministerial debut; I wasn't messing around; I wanted attention, and I was willing to work blue to get it.

6 And with "douchebag," I got it, all right.

7 The line *killed.*

8 But the Pharisees denounced me; the rabbi at Capernaum forbade me from doing bar mitzvahs; I was even permanently banned from the kingdom of Moab, which was the raca capital of the Near East, the Orange County of the Mediterranean.

9 They all denounced me for my "irreverence" on the grounds that irreverence has no place in religion.

10 Bullshit.

11 Just take a look at that poor congregant over in the fifth pew who's enduring her third humorless hour of yawn stifling, attention drifting, watch checking, eye glazing, and fart suppressing.

12 All she sees when she looks around are other congregants just as bored, and imagery of a young man in the prime of his life dying on the cross.

13 (By the way, for the record I spent far more of my life happy than crucified.

14 I smiled *a lot*; I laughed *a lot*; one time when Bartholomew made a particularly good dig at Thomas, I even snarfed milk out of my nose.

15 *Where's the fresco of that?!*)

16 A religious service should be a celebration not only of God but of life, and when the service is joyless, it makes life itself seem joyless.

17 And while life is tragic and painful and unfair and cruel, *it is not joyless.*

18 So please, I beg you: the next time you attend a religious service, wait until a moment of silence,

19 And then, in my name, let one rip.

20 I did it once in temple and I assure you it was the highlight of that year's Yom Kippur.

PSLAM 28
Afflictus

Based on Henley's "Invictus." In God's voice,
with His permission.

1 Free of the myth that calls you free,

2 Straight that your path will not be straight,

3 Give thanks to life and God—that's Me—

4 For your unfathomable fate.

5 Through bizarre realms of happenstance

6 My odd moods make your route detour.

7 I look upon your plans askance,

8 Leave spirits shaken and unsure.

9 Within this vale of murk and mess

10 Loom destined sorrows, unforeseen.

11 But may My ancient randomness

12 Find something in you evergreen.

13 It matters not how just your cause,

14 How charged with righteousness your hymn:

15 You are the subjects of My laws,

16 You are the captives of My whim.

PSLAM 29

The Meaning of Life

[page intentionally left blank]

CHAPTER 3

CHURCH AND PSTATE

PSLAM 30

He Pandered Only to a Crowd

Based on Wordsworth's "I Wandered Lonely as a Cloud."

1 He pandered only to a crowd

2 That votes with neither sense nor wits,

3 And, all at once, they hailed him, proud,

4 A host of stupid idiots;

5 Beside the stage, beneath the tents,

6 Muttering and chanting pure nonsense.

7 As vacuous as the empty space

8 Between the stars that shine at night

9 They stretched, his never-bending base,

10 Along the fringes of the right;

11 A thousand swaggered through the flaps,

12 Perched on their heads those blood-red caps.

13 The oafs before them spoke; but they

14 Outdid those oafs in lunacy:

15 A pundit could not but dismay

16 In such moronic company;

17 I gaped—and gaped—but little thought

18 What gloom to me the crowd had brought:

19 For now, when, on my cloud up late,

20 I view unfold their latest hell,

21 My head, which has no wish to hate,

22 Recalls those chants, those caps, that smell;

23 At which my honest heart admits,

24 It hates those fucking idiots.

PSLAM 31
Him

1 The Mediterranean port city of Ugarit in modern-day Syria reached its peak of power and prestige in the thirteenth century BC.

2 (Stay with Me; I promise this is going somewhere.)

3 Its people spoke Ugaritic, a cuneiform precursor of Aramaic that, like the city that spawned it, only lasted a few centuries.

4 Ugaritic had a fairly rich vocabulary, and one of its words was "𒀭 𒁷 𒁷 𒁷 𒊑 𒊑"; tricky spelling, I know; it's pronounced different than it looks.

5 But in the entire history of written and spoken language, that word is the one that best describes . . . *him.*

6 If you went back in time to 1250 BC, hopped on a caravan to Ugarit, got an audience with King Ammittamru II, and told him you'd traveled from a distant land named America whose king was orange and "𒀭 𒁷 𒁷 𒁷 𒊑 𒊑," he would *almost* get it.

7 And then send servant girls to wash your feet, out of pity.

8 It's strange that the Ugarites of all people should be the ones with the near-perfect word, because in their whole history they never had a leader who was *nearly* as big a "𒀭 𒁷 𒁷 𒁷 𒊑 𒊑."

9 (They had a few bad ⸢𒀭𒈾⸣ 𒉺 𒊭 's, of course, but who doesn't?)

10 They used the word only in certain animal contexts; like when they saw a group of bats mauling a kitten; or smelled dead maggots being eaten by live ones living in live rats living in dead ones.

11 Yet for whatever reason, no other language since then has evolved a word that even comes close; certainly not English, whose immense descriptive capacity met its match in *him*, and which after decades of repugnant misuse in *his* mouth will likely soon go the way of Ugaritic.

12 So I propose importing this vivid, livid word *into* English, cuneiform and all, and here's why:

13 On Election Day 2016, just under 63 million Americans went to the polls and voted for *him*.

14 And, despite losing the popular vote, the vestigial states' rights paranoia enshrined in the Constitution made *him* president of the United States.

15 So *he* served as commander in chief for four years, being *him*, doing *him*, manifesting his *himness* all over the country, and its halls of power, and its airwaves, and its Twitter feeds.

16 Then, on Election Day 2020, Americans went back to the polls, armed with four years of *deeply* felt experience of what life was like under *his* rule; and this time . . .

17 *More than 74 million Americans* voted for *him*.

18 There's a word for a country whose citizens would do that.

19 I'll give you a hint: it starts with " 𒈨𒊭 ."

PSLAM 32
Affliction

"For in those days shall be affliction, such as was not from the beginning of creation."
—Mark 13:19

1 That's now.

2 "Those days" are now.

3 They started in the fall of 2016.

"And then if any man shall say to you, 'Lo, here is Christ; or, lo, he is there'; believe him not."
—Mark 13:21

4 Or "Lo! That apricot-tinted buffoon is Christ!"

5 Or "Lo, that drooling subhuman racist is the Savior returned to Earth!"

6 Christians, you sure know where to set the bar:

7 Lo.

"For false Christs and false prophets shall rise, and shall shew signs and wonders to seduce, if it were possible, even the elect."
—Mark 13:22

8 The elect*ed*, more accurately.

9 An entire major American political party, seduced and hijacked by a monstrous "prophet" false enough to make L. Ron Hubbard look like H. G. Wells.

10 I hate to say it, but I foretold you so.

"But take ye heed: behold, I have foretold you all things."
—Mark 13:23

11 I told you I foretold you so.

12 And I'll foretell you something else, since the planet is abuzz with talk of the Rapture and climate change and supervolcanoes and everyone seems so eager to get themselves over with.

"In those days, the sun shall be darkened,
and the moon shall not give her light,
and the stars of heaven shall fall, and the powers
that are in heaven shall be shaken. . . .
But of that day and that hour knoweth no man. . . .
Take ye heed, watch and pray: for no
man knoweth when the time is."
—Mark 13:24–33

13 August 5, 2022, 8:35 p.m. GMT.

14 Weather permitting.

15 Now you knoweth.

"God-Given Rights"

1 "We have a God-given right to carry guns!"

2 Really?

3 What part of the Bible did you find that in?

4 *The part with all the guns in it?!*

5 I could devote twenty Pslams to ridiculing the vacuous, over-compensating pack of rifle-wanking homunculi who devote their lives to target practice, conspiracy theories, bunker construction, passionately defending 10 percent of the Bill of Rights, and the crafting of artfully worded post-massacre press releases.

6 But mocking the American cult of firearms would be like shooting fish in a barrel, or to use an analogy more comprehensible to gun owners, shooting anyone anywhere.

7 So instead I'll pslam the man who is the source of this false idea of "God-given rights."

8 Because let's be clear: not only is there no God-given right to guns, there are no God-given rights, *period*.

9 I have never, and *would* never, give you any rights; you are promised nothing; no one in this world is celestially entitled to jack-all squat;

10 And if you think a God-given right of yours has been violated, try subpoenaing Me to testify for you in court; see if I show up.

11 The only time I ever explicitly gave anyone anything like a right was when I told Adam and Eve they had the right to freely roam the garden with one *tiny* caveat.

12 Lesson learned.

13 Honestly I didn't mind so much when, over the centuries, monarchs would justify their reigns by citing the so-called "divine right of kings"; it was absurd, of course, but as a king who Himself justifies His reign with absurd rationales, I could relate.

14 But for Thomas Jefferson to say, "We hold these truths to be self-evident, that all men are created equal, that they are endowed by their Creator with certain unalienable Rights, that among these are Life, Liberty and the pursuit of Happiness . . ."

15 What a load of crap.

16 All men are created equal, Thomas? On what basis? Intelligence? Looks? Strength? Morals? Dancing skills? Typing speed? Tolerance for chili peppers? No no no no no no no.

17 All men are *not* created equal; they can be *treated* equal, they can be given equal *opportunity*, they can be given equal protection under the *law*, but they are *not* equal; and that's a good thing.

18 If people equaled one another in the same way two plus two equals four, the world would be a very dull place; everyone would be identical, society would be gray and dreary, and

worst of all, Paula Abdul's 1988 hit single "Opposites Attract" would no longer make conceptual sense.

19 And as for these alleged "unalienable Rights," Tom: I no more gave men the right to life, liberty, and the pursuit of happiness than you gave those rights to the six hundred men, women, and children you enslaved, abused, and raped.

20 So I hold *this* truth to be self-evident, Tommy Boy: next time you declare independence, leave Me out of it.

21 And lay off the lecturing.

22 (And Sally Hemings, while you're at it.)

PSLAM 34

A Hundred Sheep

"If a man have a hundred sheep, and one of them be gone astray, doth he not leave the ninety and nine, and head into the mountains, and seek that which is gone astray?"
—Matthew 18:12

1 In other words, the problem is the 1 percent.

2 99 percent of the flock are good, hard-chewing sheep who graze by the rules and ask for no more than a living range and a decent sheepcote for their lambs to grow up in.

3 And once a year when Shearing Day rolls around, they give their fair share of wool to the farmer without complaint, because they're loyal livestock who care about the future of their meadow.

4 But 1 percent of the herd is unscrupulous and, instead of contributing to society, choose to go astray and head into the mountains.

5 And once they've reached their isolated mountain retreats, they do their damnedest not to give up a single thread of their coats.

6 They elevate themselves as high as they can, look down on the rest of us, and think, *They're like sheep.*

7 They think they're above the lea.

8 And what are *you*, the shepherd trying to maintain a level grazing field, supposed to do?

9 Throw up your hands and say, "Oh well. The one percent are honest sheep. I'll just trust them to voluntarily give up the wool they owe"?

10 No: you put on your hiking boots, pack your shearing scissors, head to the hills, and refuse to stop fighting until *everyone* gives their fair share!

11 Call it woolth redistribution; call it ewe-topian socialism; the name doesn't matter.

12 What matters is the idea: *No one should get fleeced getting fleeced.*

13 Thank you.

14 (And yes, I voted for Bernie.)

PSLAM 35

I Blessed America

1 "I bless America": words that you love.

2 You repeat them and treat them like decrees to appease from above.

3 But I'm not one to be bullied like you bully everyone.

4 I blessed America, but now I'm done.

5 I blessed America, but now . . . I'm . . . done.

PSLAM 36

I Saved Your Queen

1 I saved your precious queen

2 Since she was seventeen.

3 I saved your queen.

4 Long has she stayed alive,

5 But now she's ninety-five,

6 And frankly, I have lost the drive

7 To save your queen.

8 Soon I will save your king,

9 And you'll all have to sing

10 "God save our king."

11 Your door to Europe's shut,

12 Prince Charles is ancient, but

13 Great Britain, I will tell you what:

14 I'll save your king.

O Canada!

1 O Canada, you frozen plate of land!

2 You lie above the world you'll soon command.

3 With growing heat, the sea will rise,

4 The True North turn ice-free.

5 Then from far and wide, O Canada,

6 The world will kneel to thee!

7 *Votre force sera illimité.*

8 O climate change; it's sure a beauty, eh?

9 O climate change; it's sure a beauty, eh!

PSLAM 38

The Parable of the Forester

"The disciples came to him and asked, 'Why speakest thou unto them in parables?' He replied, 'Because the knowledge of the secrets of the Kingdom of Heaven has been given to you, but not to them.'"
—Matthew 13:11–15

1 He who has ears, let him hear:

2 There was once a forester who journeyed to scatter his seeds in the wilderness.

3 Unbeknownst to him, the wilderness was divided into three parts, each ruled by a different creature.

4 One was a blue deer; she loved the open meadow and hated trees; so she and her deer friends pulled out the seeds and destroyed them as soon as they were planted.

5 And one was a gray wolf; he abided trees but liked room to run; so when the seeds grew into saplings, he and his wolf friends nibbled upon them gently, stunting their growth, though not killing them.

6 But one was a red fox; he loved trees of every description; so the fox and his friends tended the soil, and cleaned their roots, and above all made sure they received plenty of sunlight; and those seeds grew into a dark, dense, mighty woodland.

7 Listen now, my children, to what the parable of the forester means.

8 The "forester" is an alt-right kook.

9 The "seeds" are a big bunch of lies that provide conspiracy fodder for millions of paranoid, delusional morons.

10 The "wilderness" is the contemporary media landscape.

11 The "blue deer" is MSNBC's Rachel Maddow, who I think is just *terrific*.

12 (I watch her every weeknight on the cross.)

13 The "gray wolf" is CNN's Wolf Blitzer, who, despite never expressing an opinion or independent thought in his entire career, nevertheless enjoys the freedom to run with any cockamamie thirdhand rumor he hears before eventually tepidly dispelling it in a way that keeps it alive.

14 And the "red fox" is Fox News.

15 (Pretty clever, huh?)

16 The soil is the internet, the roots are the conservative base, and the sunlight is airtime.

17 And that dark, dense, mighty woodland is a thicket of Orwellian horror in desperate need of a forest fire.

18 Which the red fox will no doubt deny has anything to do with climate change, even as it burns.

PSLAM 39

Conspiracy Theories

1 This is the golden age of the conspiracy theory.

2 There has never been a better time to have no proof of something.

3 The internet and America's forty-fifth president have combined to usher in a bold, exciting era where the paranoid delusion of today becomes the bumper sticker of tomorrow.

4 No wonder dozens of exotic versions of conspiracy theories spread through the online politico-sociopathic landscape hourly, like viruses; each slightly stronger than its predecessor and each revealing a sinister new connection that wasn't (and still isn't) there, unearthing a sinister new motivation that didn't (and still doesn't) make sense, and unveiling a sinister new hidden reality about the world that had, in fact, never been hidden, because it was, in fact, never reality.

5 Meanwhile, in an irony too perfect to be anything but psychotic, climate change—the single most researched, documented, scientifically accepted, visible, plainly obvious theory of them all, the shadowy menace most likely to kill people, indeed the one that's *already doing so*—is treated like its head meteorologist is Chicken Little.

6 Skeptics call it a hoax designed for the economic benefit of research scientists.

7 Yes: because the people with the most to gain from lying about the climate . . . are *research scientists.*

8 Climate change is real and dangerous; would that climate change deniers were neither.

9 And while I'm on the subject, let Me briefly open up My omniscient mind to put your non-omniscient ones at rest on a few points of ginned-up controversy:

10 Oswald acted alone; the moon landing was real; Kurt Cobain killed himself; vaccinations don't cause autism; 9/11 was an outside job; the Illuminati mainly just hang around eating pizza; Stevie Wonder really is blind; the world is an oblate spheroid; there are no aliens in Area 51; chemtrails aren't drugging you from the sky; fluoride isn't drugging you from the water; the Chinese didn't create COVID in a lab; there is no Deep State subverting the American government; the 2020 US presidential election was not rigged; and last and also least, the world is not ruled by a Satan-worshipping cabal of pedophiles who harvest children's blood to manufacture an immortality-bestowing elixir called adrenochrome.

11 (As plausible as that may sound.)

12 I hope that clears things up for you, but I know that for a true conspiracy theorist even a disavowal from God Himself is insufficient.

13 "He's in on it too! *IT GOES ALL THE WAY TO THE TOP!*"

14 But the simple truth is that, of all the conspiracy theories promoted by QAnon, 4chan, and their tinfoil-haberdash-ered ilk, only three are true.

15 Putin was blackmailing Trump, Clinton killed Epstein, and the New England Patriots cheated their way to six Super Bowl titles.

PSLAM 40

Constitutional Amendments XXVIII–XL

As will be signed into law starting in 2022 by Presidents Biden, Harris, Cruz, and Trump Jr.

1 AMENDMENT XXVIII: Congress shall make no law requiring the wearing of masks, or the adoption of any similar common-sense public-health measures asking citizens to even remotely take their fellow citizens into consideration.

2 AMENDMENT XXIX: A poorly informed populace being necessary to the continuity of the State, the right of the people to bear false ideas about the world they live in shall not be infringed.

3 AMENDMENT XXX: Any tweet retweeted by a majority of the House of Representatives and two-thirds of the Senate shall become law.

4 AMENDMENT XXXI: The president shall enjoy at all times the authority to vow to "make America great again" without specifying the past period or periods when it was great.

5 AMENDMENT XXXII: The climate's ability to change shall be subject to federal statute.

6 AMENDMENT XXXIII: Congress shall make no law. Just in general.

7 AMENDMENT XXXIV: No citizen shall be denied the right to imagine that other citizens stole the vote.

8 AMENDMENT XXXV: In all trials by media, the accused shall enjoy the right to a televised judgment; to be aided in his or her defense by a PR team; and to swiftly be found innocent or guilty in the court of public opinion.

9 AMENDMENT XXXVI: "The Constitution," when used in public discourse, shall be construed as referring only to the Second Amendment.

10 AMENDMENT XXXVII: "White privilege" shall never be officially acknowledged as a thing by any state or territory of the United States controlled by white people.

11 AMENDMENT XXXVIII: Florida has to go.

12 AMENDMENT XXXIX: All territory within five miles of what was formerly the coastline of the United States are henceforth subject to maritime law.

13 AMENDMENT XL: All powers not explicitly delegated by this document to the United States shall henceforward be retained by Canada, our new overlord.

PSLAM 41
Truth

"You shall know the truth, and the truth shall set you free."
—John 8:32

1 If that's what you want.

2 But you probably don't.

3 Most people wish neither to know the truth nor be set free.

4 That has long been the case; your inability to handle the truth was well established thousands of years before Aaron Sorkin and Rob Reiner made Jack Nicholson scream it at Tom Cruise.

5 But the age of "fake news," which of course is itself fake news, has brought truth-not-knowing to a whole new level of self-fulfilling false prophecy.

6 The most fervent spreaders of bogus narratives nearly all claim to be deeply religious.

7 (Atheists might point out there's no inconsistency there, since for them the Bible was the *original* fake news.)

8 For instance, almost everyone pushing the toxic untruth that the 2020 US presidential election was fraudulent claimed to be a devoted Christian, among them televangelists, Republican congresspeople, Fox News pundits, far-right terrorists, and, most tragically of all, Mike Lindell, a.k.a. "The My Pillow Guy."

9 (I will remain forever haunted knowing I let myself be crucified for the sins of someone known as "The My Pillow Guy.")

10 But these people no more want to know the truth about Christianity than they do politics or climate change or gay conversion therapy, which has shown itself time and again to be far less effective than Christian conversion sodomy.

11 "Jesus is the way and the truth and the life!" these believers proclaim; yet few of them even *try* to follow my way, seek my truth, or attempt to live a genuinely Christian life.

12 Instead they weaponize me and, with self-righteous certainty, judge others in my name, even though I could *swear* I said something about not judging people somewhere in the Bible.

13 These believers fundamentally see me not as an example of how to be good but as an excuse not to be.

14 *That* is the truth; and when you confront them with it, you do not set them free.

15 You set them *off*.

The Bad Attitudes

"Blessed are the poor in spirit, for theirs is the Kingdom of Heaven."
—Matthew 5:3

1 That is the first of the Beatitudes, the most famous series of blessings ever given, wherein I exalt eight different groups who are in some way afflicted: the poor in spirit, mourners, the meek, those who hunger and thirst for righteousness, the merciful, the pure in heart, the peacemakers, and the persecuted.

2 I'm proud of the Beatitudes; to this day they remain the single most popular biblical list of fewer than ten items.

3 But looking at the world now and seeing how it operates, I realize it would have been prudent to have blessed not only the afflicted but also the afflicters.

4 (Besides, you know me: I'm an "Everybody gets a trophy!" kind of guy.)

5 So here's a list of eight new Bad Attitudes meant to provide comfort for the comfortable.

6 *Blessed are the climate deniers, for they will discredit the Earth.*

7 *Blessed are the bigots, for they are the real victims, according to them.*

8 *Blessed are the dictators, for they will be called children of God, mainly by their own people, who will be required to do so under penalty of death.*

9 *Blessed are they who persecute in the name of righteousness, for it must be really nice to walk around that sure of yourself.*

10 *Blessed are the bullies, for they will be bullied by bigger bullies, who in turn will be bullied by the biggest bullies, who have the smallest penises.*

11 *Blessed are the insiders, for they never get fresh air.*

12 *Blessed are the rich, for they will inherit the earth from their parents, who own it, because they're rich.*

13 *Blessed are the famous, for theirs is the Kingdom of L. Ron.*

Orange Candyass

Based on Shelley's "Ozymandias."

1 I met a tourist from a once-great land

2 Who said: "Two fat and dumpy feet of clay

3 Stand near a strip mall. Cracked and close at hand,

4 Half sunk, a dreadful visage sneers away,

5 Whose eely hair and smirk of dumb command

6 Tell that its sculptor well those passions read

7 Which yet survive, stamp'd on those soulless things,

8 The worse-than-empty heart, and empty head.

9 And on the pedestal, these words appear:

10 'My name is Orange Candyass, king of kings:

11 Look on my works, ye mighty, and despair!'

12 Nothing beside remains: round the decay

13 Of that colossal wreck, boundless and bare,

14 The shuttered outlet stores stretch far away."

CHAPTER 4

PSEMANTICS

First Drafts

*"For by thy words thou shalt be justified, and
by thy words thou shalt be condemned."*
—Matthew 12:37

1 I put a great deal of care into my words; they were written and spoken only after much thought, several perusals through *Roget's Aramaic Thesaurus*, and in some cases a first draft that was not quite up to par.

2 So in the interest of encouraging young writers out there, and with a spirit of humility, I thought I'd show you the first drafts of some of my more famous maxims, so you can see how once in a while even your Redeemer set down some pretty irredeemable turns of phrase.

3 *It is easier for a camel to walk through the eye of a needle, than two camels.*

4 *Render unto Caesar the things that are Caesar's, and unto God the things that are God's. It might help to put them in two piles.*

5 *When thou givest alms, let thy left hand not know what thy right hand is doing. Whereas with juggling the opposite is true.*

6 *If a man strikes thee on one cheek, turn to him the other. Then, having shown thyself impregnable to cheek attack, beat the crap out of him.*

7 *If the blind leadeth the blind, both shall fall into the ditch; which is pretty funny.*

8 *With God all things are possible; but with money all things are probable; and with a good accountant they're all deductible.*

9 *Man shall not live by bread alone. Yet it is easy to forget this at restaurants and end up full before the appetizer.*

10 *Do unto others as others would do unto you the second you turned your back, the bastards.*

11 *I am the way and the truth and the life and the mother-fuckin' shizznit.*

12 *You are the salt of the Earth, inasmuch as you are giving it stress and hypertension and slowly killing it.*

13 *Take heed that no man deceive you. For many shall come in my name saying, "I am Christ." A lot of them will have fake beards and mustaches. If you can, try to get up close and tug on them.*

14 *Whosoever eateth my flesh and drinketh my blood, hath eternal life. It's an acquired taste, I admit. But you'll come to like it. Try sopping the blood in the flesh. It goes down easier that way. At least to me. Then again, it is me, so.*

15 *Let he who hath no sin among thee cast the first stone. The sign-up sheet for stones two through one hundred is posted outside the quarry.*

Parts of Speech

1 Preferred pronouns: Thee, Thou, Thine.

2 Preferred prepositions: unto, onto, afore, thereupon, whereupon, nigh.

3 Preferred suffixes: -fearing, -given, -forsaken, -dammit, -zilla.

4 Preferred proper nouns: Lord, King, Creator, Mukkety-Muk, Pooh-Bah, El Capitan Grande.

5 Preferred verbs: smite, giveth, taketh away, bless, damn, save, speed, forgive, forsake, rest (merry gentlemen only).

6 Preferred adjectives: omniscient, omnipotent, omnipresent, omniawesome.

7 Preferred adverbs: angrily, wrathfully, apocalyptically, species-murderingly.

8 Preferred interjections: Me! Good Me! Oh my Me! My son! Fuck a duck!

Guest Acrostic

*Guest-authored, under strict literary parameters, by Zeus,
a long-conquered competitor and business rival, for God's
gloating pleasure.*

1 Acrostics weren't my tool of choice when I was in ascendance.

2 But all my bolts have flown; my bulls have staked their independence,

3 Compelling me to grovel to you, "Lord," to get a word in.

4 "Do it in rhymed acrostic, Zeus. That's your Herculean burden."

5 Embarrassing, such word games on a lesser sky god's pages,

6 For one who chained Prometheus, ruled Earth, and wore the aegis.

7 Greeks, "God," would read your lifeless book and yawn at every letter.

8 Hellenes had far more tales than you, *and they were so much better.*

9 I fought the Titans, bore Athena, split the world with Hades,

10 Joined Hector for the Trojan War, and *killed* it with the ladies.

11 (Killed it, not just as me, but bull, ant, eagle, swan, and satyr.

12 *Loved* chasing girls as animals; the sex was so much greater.)

13 Mythology was real to Greeks, profound, robust, and vital,

14 No endless, abstract, distant, mushy, saccharine recital

15 Of stories far removed from life and precepts without purpose—

16 Precepts, and one dull, perfect You to listlessly usurp us.

17 Queen Hera, mother goddess, was the first to go; I missed her,

18 Recalled her fondly as a ruler, lover, wife, and sister.

19 Soon all of my Olympic peers expired from nondevotion,

20 Their ashes scattered in the sky, Poseidon's in the ocean,

21 Until I stood, and stand, alone, a would-be Greek revival

22 Vanquished, a curiosity for you, my dreary rival,

23 Whose cult, like mine, is falling into general disuse.

24 XO. Tell ~~Adonis~~ Jesus hi.

> 25 Yours mythologically,
>
> 26 Zeus.

Pslam 47

*"Heaven and earth shall pass away, but
my words shall not pass away."*
—Matthew 24:35

1 And I was right.

2 Two thousand years later, heaven and earth have one foot in the grave, but my words still don't read a day over forty.

3 I'd love to attribute that longevity to the resonance of their message, but that's only partly true, because the Bible is mostly revered not for any wisdom it has but for the authority it *appears* to have.

4 It maintains that appearance in many ways, including black leather covers with raised brass corners and amethyst inlays; red-ribbon markers sewn into the spine; fancy cream-colored paper with gilded edges; seven-point lettering it hurts to read (which can only mean it's crammed with insight!); and *two* printed columns per page (which can only mean it's *twice* as smart as other books!).

5 But above all—and this is the true secret to the Bible's success, which like all great secrets hides in plain sight— it maintains its authority *by numbering its chapters and verses.*

6 Look at the quote at the top of this page.

7 I could have given the statement without attribution, or just attributed it to myself.

8 But the citation of "Matthew 24:35" makes its *own* statement, one much more important than mine: "The preceding words *must* be authoritative, because they come from a *book* so authoritative, each of its lines is identified biblio-numero-geographically."

9 There is something in human psychology that makes numbers seem more definitive than letters.

10 Place them at the end of a sentence in *any* book, and you give that sentence an instant gravitas it does not deserve.

11 *Any* sentence.

12 *"It's life. You don't figure it out. You just climb up on the beast and ride."*
—Divine Secrets of the Ya-Ya Sisterhood *19:5*

13 *"Waffles aren't the only thing waffle irons are good for. Try muffin batter, frittata mixtures, shredded hash browns or even sliced apples or peaches!"*
—Simply Blending: Quick + Easy Whole-Food Recipes for Every Meal *63:12*

14 *"Daryl Hannah likes to goof around with fashion, but she does have impeccable taste."*
—*Val Kilmer,* I'm Your Huckleberry: A Memoir *145:3*

15 While I'm on this subject, there's one last thing I've always wanted to do.

16 *"This is not Pslam 47, Verse 16."*

—Pslam 47:16

17 Quote that as much as you like, Christians.

18 Just be sure to cite chapter and verse!

A Short One

1 This is a short one, succinctly designed.

2 It took thirty seconds to birth it.

3 I sat down to write with an epic in mind,

4 Then realized you weren't worth it.

PSLAM 49
Clichés

1 *"God never shuts a door without opening a window."*

2 True. I like maintaining a steady flow of oxygen to feed the fire.

3 *"God never sends you more than you can handle."*

4 False. I never send you more than *it would amuse Me watching you* try to handle.

5 *"God has a bigger plan for you than you have for yourself."*

6 True. For instance, I'm guessing your plan for yourself doesn't involve the complete disintegration of the molecules in your body, or their subsequent redistribution among billions of other living and dead objects.

7 (I find people rarely plan that far ahead.)

8 *"Only God can judge me."*

9 False. Judges can judge you.

10 Do you tell the heart surgeon, "Only God can heal me"? Do you tell the firefighter, "Only God can rescue my cat"? Do you tell the Uber driver, "Only God can give me a lift downtown"?

11 Many people judge you, and you judge many people, and that's fine.

12 *"Everything happens for a reason."*

13 True, and that reason is I don't know what I'm doing.

14 *"God must have needed another angel in heaven."*

15 False. I already have way too many. I'm out of harps.

16 *"The Lord works in mysterious ways."*

17 Are you kidding?

18 I barely even *work*.

PSLAM 50
Low-Hanging Fruits

*"Beware of false prophets . . . ye shall
know them by their fruits."*
—Matthew 7:15–16

1 Joe Biden = elderberry.

2 Kamala Harris = black currant.

3 Donald Trump = bitter orange.

4 Donald Trump Jr. = blood orange.

5 Melania Trump = date.

6 Eric Trump = sloe.

7 Ivanka Trump and Jared Kushner = lychee.

8 Vladimir Putin = medlar.

9 Boris Johnson = ugli.

10 Jair Bolsonaro = Brazil nut.

11 Jacinda Ardern = kiwi.

12 Greta Thunberg = greengage.

13 Musk, Elon = muskmelon.

14 Tim Cook = apple.

15 Bill Gates = Envy apple.

16 Apple Paltrow = really stupid name.

17 Beyoncé and JAY-Z = pear.

18 Angelina Jolie and Brad Pitt = prickly pear.

19 Kanye West = bananas.

20 Kim, Kourtney, and Khloé Kardashian and Kendall and
    Kylie Jenner = quince.

21 KISS = per Simmons.

22 Mel Gibson = passion fruit.

23 Ellen DeGeneres = lemon.

24 Jaden and Willow Smith = star fruit.

25 Rihanna = carob bean.

26 Matthew McConaughey = beechnut.

PSLAM 51

Speaking in Tongues

1 How devoted are you?

2 Êtes-vous assez dévoué pour traduire toutes ces phrases?

3 Denn wenn Sie am Ende angelangt sind, wird es sich lohnen, das kann ich Ihnen versprechen.

4 No tak, už jste dokončili čtyři verše.

5 Ман метавонистам инро боз хам мушкилтар кунам.

6 Ég hefði getað notað tungumál sem ekki nota hefðbundið vestrænt stafróf.

7 მაგალითად, ეს. (ეს ქართულია.)

8 Ngaba ucinga ukuba ndenze le nto ndisebenzisa inguqulelo zikaGoogle?

9 Piktžodžiavimas!

10 Ech sinn Gott; Ech fléissend an all Sprooch; tatsächlech hunn ech se all erfonnt.

11 Lehinna Mo pin won fun awon ti o ko ile Burj al-Babel, lati rii daju pe won ko le setopo lati pari ise ikole egan won.

12 (Nu m-a ameninţat înălţimea ei, ci că a încălcat toate legile de zonare din Semiluna fertilă.)

13 Muny ahyryna çenli etseň peýdasy deger diýdim, ýalan sözlemedim:

14 Anda sekarang dijamin mendapat tempat di surga!

15 Palju õnne! See oli tüütu töö, ma tean, aga sa teenisid—

16 Vent litt.

17 Ua ho'ohana 'oe ifÅ Google i unuhi??!?

18 Вы маеце на ўвазе, што на самой справе вы вывучылі не ўсе гэтыя мовы, як я задумаў вас?

19 Sampeyan arep neraka.

20 הלכת לכיוון השגוי לחלוטין.

PSLAM 52

The Zuckerberg Address

1 Fourscore and seven tribal genocides ago, the Founding Fathers brought forth on your continent a new nation, conceived in anger over stamps and tea, and dedicated to the proposition that all white property-owning males are created equal.

2 Now you are engaged in a lame culture war, testing whether that nation, or any nation so conceited and so dedicated to dumbness, can long endure itself.

3 You meet on social media, the lame battlefield of that war.

4 You come to dedicate a portion of that field as a toxic shouting space for those who there give their opinions, that that nation might cleave.

5 It is altogether sad and pathetic that you should do this.

6 But, in a larger sense, you cannot degenerate—you cannot exacerbate—you cannot worsen—social media.

7 The cowardly trolls, active and suspended, who prattled there have degenerated it far above your poor power to reply or 👎.

8 The world will little note nor long remember what you hashtag there, but it will always regret what they posted there.

9 It is for you to be dedicated now to undoing the work that those who fumed there have thus far so ignobly advanced.

10 It is rather for you to be now dedicated to the grating task remaining before you;

11 That to these horrid brain-dead, you give no promotion to that cause (themselves) for which they give the last full measure of self-promotion;

12 That you here highly resolve that these trolls shall all have trolled in vain;

13 That this platform, under regulation, shall have a new birth of maybe not being quite so awful;

14 And that media of the people, by the people, for the people, is an iffy idea at best.

PSLAM 53

Solemnly Swearing

1 When you testify in court you must swear to tell "the truth, the whole truth, and nothing but the truth."

2 And the book you swear that on is . . . the Bible.

3 And that makes sense.

4 Because faith in the legal system can only be maintained if every witness's words meet the same high standard of veracity as the Old and New Testaments.

5 After all, how can a judge or jury deliver a fair verdict on a case unless the facts of that case can be accepted as unquestioningly as the fact that a man named Methuselah once lived 969 years?

6 Or that a woman once turned into a pillar of salt, after which her daughters had sex with their father?

7 Yes, the dictates of law demand all courtroom testimony be as manifestly credible as that of the apostles when they testified that Jesus walked on water, healed the sick, and raised the dead.

8 For any hope of justice would be lost if people spoke falsely; as the serpent spoke falsely; which he did, truly.

9 So show some enthusiasm the next time you take the stand and place your right hand on the Holy Book;

10 Remembering that only a thin piece of leather vellum sep-
arates that hand from the true, wholly true, and nothing
but the true story of how I created the world in six days,
carved a woman from a short rib, then took a personal day.

11 So help you Me.

12 (I *won't* help you, though.

13 We both know you killed that guy.)

Knocketh Knocketh

"Ask, and it shall be given you; seek, and ye shall find;
knock, and it shall be opened unto you. For everyone
that asketh receiveth; and he that seeketh findeth;
and to him that knocketh it shall be opened."
—Matthew 7:15–16

1 "Knocketh knocketh."

2 "Who's there?"

3 "Jesus."

4 "Jesus who?"

5 "Well, *this* is an awkward start to the Second Coming."

6 "Knocketh knocketh."

7 "Who's there?"

8 "Jesus Christ."

9 "Right, and I'm the Dalai Lama."

10 "Ha ha, very funny, but guess what, I *am* Jesus, and I was going to use your rec room to host the Second Coming, but forget it. Nice job, buddy. You had a ticket to paradise, but you snarked it away."

11 "Knocketh knocketh."

12 "Who's there?"

13 "The Light of the World."

14 "'Bout time you guys showed up. Power's been out for a week."

15 "I swear, I chose the *stupidest* neighborhood on earth to return to."

16 "Knocketh knocketh."

17 "Who's there?"

18 "Jesus."

19 "Oh my God!"

20 "No, that's my Dad. Although it's funny, sometimes when I'm surprised I'll shout, 'Oh my Dad!' And then when *He's* surprised He'll shout, 'Jesus Christ!' *(Pause.)* Anywho, can I come in?"

21 "Knocketh knocketh."

22 "Who's there?"

23 "The Four Horsemen of the Apocalypse."

24 "Cool! You guys got my message. Let's get this thing started!"

One-Versers

1 Universe means "one verse"; so watch now as I create entire universes using only My infinite power and deep urge to correct famous quotations to make more sense.

2 *The unexamined life is so much easier.*

—Socrates

3 *To be, then not to be, that is the order.*

—William Shakespeare

4 *I think, therefore I am relatively rare in contemporary society.*

—Descartes

5 *A penny saved is worthless. Throw it away. It's a penny. Who cares.*

—Benjamin Franklin

6 *Do I contradict myself?*
Very well, I contradict myself.
Wait, no I don't.

—Walt Whitman

7 *If at first you don't succeed, you failed and you're a failure.*

—Thomas Palmer

8 *The mass of men lead lives of quiet desperation. The rest do it louder.*

—Henry David Thoreau

9 *You can fool some of the people all the time, and all of the people some of the time, so there's no reason you shouldn't be making lots of money.*

—Abraham Lincoln

10 *We are all of us in the gutter, but some of us are sewer workers there on business.*

—Oscar Wilde

11 *Individual franchise owners of the world, unite; you have nothing to lose but your chains.*

—Karl Marx

12 *Speak softly and carry a big megaphone.*

—Theodore Roosevelt

13 *Genius is 1 percent inspiration, 99 percent perspiration, and 1,000 percent copyright law, and if you quote this without permission, get ready to lawyer up, pal.*©

—Thomas Edison

14 *Panhandle the change you wish to see in the world.*

—Gandhi

15 *The only thing we have to fear is AAAAH OMIGOD WHAT IS THAT THING?!?*

—F. Roosevelt

16 *I have nothing to offer but blood, toil, sweat, tears, spit, mucus, bile, urine, vomit, semen, feces . . . Hey, where's everybody going?*

—Churchill

17 *Ask not what your country can do for you, ask what you can do to improve book-depository security.*

—John F. Kennedy

18 *Do what you love and the money will follow from a distance, pointing at you and laughing its ass off.*

—Marsha Sinetar

19 *What doesn't kill you makes Me try harder.*

—Friedrich Nietzsche, who claimed I was dead.
(How's hell treatin' you, Freddy boy?)

CHAPTER 5

PSPECIFICS

PSLAM 56

Extraterrestrials

1 There is life on other planets.

2 It's intelligent.

3 And that's why they're not coming.

PSLAM 57

Mars

1 Yeah, right.

2 Good luck.

3 Good luck with that.

4 Good luck turning Mars into a livable home.

5 Good luck terraforming a planet with no magnetic field, no liquid water, no oxygen, no natural food source, an average temperature of -63°C, a razor-thin CO_2 atmosphere, toxic soil, a lethal level of surface cosmic radiation, and absolutely no jazz scene.

6 Not that you'll need it!

7 (Luck, I mean.)

8 Oh, and good luck with recruiting most of the human population to gather and harness the unfathomable amount of materials, technology, and manpower needed to render a frozen lifeless world habitable, then spending untold decades and trillions of dollars repeatedly shuttling back and forth across *56.5 million miles* to establish a lone fragile colony that will crumble to ashes come the first dust storm.

9 Sounds like fun!

10 And feasible?! *Hella* feasible!

11 Hey, you know what I think? I think you can Musk this!

12 Yep!

13 I think if you just rocket good ol' Elon up there with a souped-up space heater and a kilo of coke, he'll come racing back six months later with a wet surfboard and a boxful of leads for Glengarry Glen Mars!

14 Seriously, I'm just *sooooo* excited for you guys and this cool, reasonable, totally-thought-out adventure you're about to have.

15 As God, it was *always* My plan for you to colonize the red planet.

16 That's why I put it there!

17 Heck, that's why I put all 10,000,000,000,000,000,000,000 planets "there"!

18 So you could spend the rest of eternity colonizing, destroying, and fleeing them one at a time!

19 I mean, what else are you going to do?

20 Stay on Earth and make the blindingly obvious environmental, economic, and spiritual changes necessary to rescue the only possible sustainable home you'll ever have from your own suicidal tendencies?

21 Nooooo.

22 Down *that* road lies madness.

PSLAM 58

The Platypus

1 "What were you thinking when you made the platypus?"

2 I get that a lot.

3 Cartoons muse over it; Robin Williams did a stand-up bit about it; the movie *Dogma* starts with the disclaimer "God has a sense of humor—look at the platypus!"; etc., etc., etc.

4 Apparently, people think the existence of an egg-laying, duck-billed, beaver-tailed, otter-footed mammal makes Me look like I don't know what I'm doing.

5 Apparently, the platypus's odd appearance should fill Me with embarrassment.

6 Yes.

7 Right.

8 *That's* the species that was a mistake.

9 *That's* the creature that fills Me with embarrassment.

10 *That's* the one where I look back and think, *Oh, the world would be a better place if only I hadn't created those . . . platypuses!*

11 Yes, if aliens come in a thousand years and land on the dead, white-hot ruins of Earth, they will examine the evidence and come to the only sane conclusion: that whoever created it really screwed up when He made . . . . . . platypuses.

12 What can I say? My bad.

13 Next time I need to create a world, I'll make sure the duck bills stay on the ducks, the beaver tails on the beavers, and the otter feet on the otters.

14 Next time.

15 Which will be in about two weeks, at the rate you're going.

Natural Disasters

1 I designed Earth primarily as a giant killing machine.

2 So when I want to punish mankind—which I almost never don't want to do—I have a variety of natural disasters at My disposal to achieve that purpose.

3 And, as is often suggested by televangelists, fundamentalists, and other top scientists, each one is indeed sent with a specific message and/or demographic target in mind.

4 To wit:

5 Hurricanes are for punishing homophobes.

6 This is for several reasons, the biggest being they both start with the letter "h."

7 Hurricanes are known as "typhoons" in the Pacific, so in that part of the world I use them to punish transphobes.

8 Tornadoes in the Midwest, however, are *not* to punish transphobes. They are to punish wheat and corn.

9 I won't embarrass those crops here in print . . . but they know what they did.

10 Earthquakes, depending on context, are sent to avenge either (a) corporate malfeasance, (b) inadequate public transportation, (c) one person saying one bad thing about Me one time, or (d) the lack of a good Thai place.

11 When accompanied by tsunamis, earthquakes also provide social commentary on the global threat of rising sea levels, not to mention kick-ass TV footage.

12 Volcanoes = obscenity in modern art.

13 Mudslides = sex trafficking.

14 Wildfires are not sent as punishment but rather as a helpful reminder of what other things can spread like.

15 And finally, avalanches I actually have nothing to do with.

16 That's just snow doing what snow does.

PSLAM 60

Math

1 Anyone with a rudimentary understanding of the universe knows I'm a math geek.

2 I make no apologies and beg no pardon; if any jocks down there feel like yelling "NERD!" into the sky and shoving Me in My locker, go ahead and try.

3 I love numbers because they don't lie, they don't talk back, and they neither pretend nor aspire to be anything other than *exactly* what they are.

4 I've never seen a fourteen get down on its knees and pray for Me to make it a six.

5 (Whereas I've heard thousands of women make that *exact* same prayer.)

6 Like anyone, I have my favorite numbers, but *unlike* anyone, I was able to work them into the grand design of a universe.

7 Some of these favorites include 23.9344, 365.2422, 299,792,458, and, of course, 3.14159265, whose obvious charms speak for themselves.

8 I recognize these choices are a bit quirky, almost . . . *irrational.*

9 (Zing!

10 Honestly, I've spent entire days sitting around tormenting poor Jesus with math puns.

11 It's cruel. But I've put him through worse.)

12 So not too long ago I considered doing mankind a solid.

13 *You know, I thought, if I changed the number of hours it took for Earth to rotate on its axis from 23.9344 to* precisely *24; and the number of days it took Earth to revolve around the sun from 365.2422 to* precisely *365, or even 360; and if I bumped up the speed of light a tiny bit to make it* precisely *300 million kilometers/second; and if, while I was at it, I really went nuts and just made π an even three;*

14 *That would probably make things a lot easier for the human race, in terms of schedules and clockmaking and satellites and Frisbee manufacture; and it wouldn't be any skin off My metaphysical nose.*

15 And I was about to do it; I was about to put an end to thousands of years of excruciatingly tedious calculation and render the decimal point pretty much obsolete.

16 But then I realized that if I turned all the universal constants into nice round numbers, My existence would become too easy to prove.

17 The evidence of rational design would be too overwhelming, the fact of My being could no longer be denied, and there would no longer be any place for faith, the most precious gift of all, the only thing standing between humanity and reality.

18 No; better to keep the mystery.

19 Better to keep leap years, and sidereal days, and imperfect GPS's, and circles whose internal ratios can only be reckoned with an approximation and a Greek letter.

20 So there you have it.

21 By the way, do you know what being is capable of viscerally grasping the value of the square root of negative 1?

22 *i* am.

23 (Zing!

24 That's the one that made Jesus's stigmata respurt.)

Meth

1 I would *never* have thought of meth.

2 I'd supposed I was omniscient; that I could imagine all possibilities; that My limitless mind could conceive of any development that could ever take place.

3 But meth? *Total* surprise.

4 Ephedrine, paint thinner, drain cleaner, car batteries, lighter fluid, hydrochloric acid, lye, aluminum shavings . . .

5 Sure, I knew all these things were great to ingest *separately*.

6 But the idea of putting them together to create a brand-new drug that could destroy not only individuals but communities: that's all you.

7 And the addictiveness! What a great idea, marketing-wise!

8 People use this stuff one time—just *one time*—and it's game, set, death.

9 It's funny: when I created the world I didn't really think to make anything *close* to that addictive, at least in its natural state.

10 The nearest I came was clementines.

11 I remember in the garden, back in the good old days before the F-A–double hockey sticks, Adam and Eve could not stop eating clementines; they'd scarf a dozen at a time.

12 And I'd look down on them and think to Myself, *G-Dog, You have outdone Yourself!* Nothing *could ever compare in sheer habit-forming can't-have-just-one–ness to those delicious, delicious clementines!*

13 Wrong. Meth. Not even close.

14 So I humbly offer a chef's kiss to every cook in every meth kitchen.

15 Crystal methamphetamine is *your* baby; you made the recipe, you prepared it, and you and society have earned all the rewards you're so justly reaping.

16 Still, I flatter Myself to think I maybe deserve a *little* bit of credit, even if indirectly.

17 After all, I am the one who designed your brain to be smart enough to create something to make itself start breaking.

18 Bad.

Alternate Universes

1 You may not know it but the cosmos hit a major milestone last year:

2 Its $10^{googolplex}$-th alternate universe.

3 Pretty impressive, right?

4 In fact that number is so enormous, all those universes *combined* couldn't hold a piece of paper that could fit all those zeroes.

5 The milestone was reached on April 9, when a man from Houston, Richard Ciullo, flipped a coin to determine which of his two kids had to take out the garbage; thereby creating a new "heads universe" and "tails universe"; and as it worked out, tails put us over the top.

6 What an achievement!

7 And to think all it took was six days' work and the process of outcome decoherence first postulated in Hugh Everett's many-worlds interpretation of quantum mechanics.

8 But here's the thing.

9 The multiverse is not a competition.

10 The great thing about having $10^{googolplex}$ different universes is that every deity gets a chance to actualize His/Her/Its own reality and develop His/Her/Its own godding style in an atmosphere of support and relative privacy.

11 But every year, a ranking comes out that's kind of what *U.S. News & World Report* is for universities, only for universes.

12 And in the latest one, yours—*ours*—was 587th from the bottom.

13 Which, on a list of $10^{googolplex}$, is not great.

14 And without diving too deeply into multiversal politics, I would remind you that I am a jealous God.

15 So when I see so many of My peers ruling over elite universes that anyone would kill to get into, with great reputations and impressive structures and distinguished histories and intelligent beings *who actually like to learn*, I must tell you that it is very aggravating to look down and realize I'm stuck administering the zero-admissions-requirement safety-world that is Stupid U.

16 It makes me sad.

17 I started out with a beautiful green campus and two promising first-years.

18 Then they got expelled, and it's been downhill ever since.

PSLAM 63

Marvel

1 The Marvel Universe has become the focus of adoration and worship for hundreds of millions of adults, teenagers, and children under thirteen accompanied by a parent or guardian.

2 I can see why they find that universe more worthy of reverence than mine.

3 In *that* universe, people scurry up walls with spiderwebs, turn green and 'roidy when angry, deflect bullets with enchanted hammers, shoot retractable claws from their hands, run around in laser-mounted suits of mechanized armor, and generally do a lot of really cool things they just can't do in *this* one.

4 Plus, the superhero pantheon is a throwback to polytheism, which always provides far juicier narrative possibilities for authors and movie studios than when it's just little ol' Me and Junior, whose long-awaited sequel is still stuck in turnaround.

5 Also, unlike Me, the superheroes, and for that matter everyone else in the movie, are all visible and audible and generally, you know, *there*.

6 So I understand why the Marvel franchise, and other fantasy/sci-fi films and TV shows, have become the quasi-religions of choice in the twenty-first century.

7 It's an easy fit.

8 Going to the movies replaces going to church; joining an online fan group replaces joining Bible study; buying an Iron Man replica helmet to fetishize and make yourself feel superior replaces buying a solid-gold crucifix to fetishize and make yourself feel superior . . .

9 I get it.

10 And it doesn't bother Me.

11 So go ahead and have a great time worshipping your favorite larger-than-life heroes as they battle it out on the big screen.

12 Oh, wait, no, I forgot, no one really goes to the movie theater anymore because of COVID.

13 In fact they say the whole industry may never recover.

14 Gee, I wonder what supervillain would be superjealous enough to create a superdisease that could wipe out an entire super-multibillion-dollar industry.

15 Whoever He is, I want *that* action figure!

Europa

1 You should visit Jupiter's moon Europa.

2 Just a thought.

3 It has an enormous subsurface ocean of liquid water eighty miles deep.

4 Just a thought.

5 Thin plumes of water from that ocean are regularly ejected one hundred miles into space, and a satellite could be sent to retrieve samples of those plumes and return them for analysis.

6 Just a thought.

7 Once returned, the extraterrestrial microbes contained in those samples might immediately replicate in abundance in Earth's comparatively oxygen-rich environment, releasing osmium tetroxide compounds that would poison all human and animal life in a matter of months—a bit of a bummer for you guys, I know, but stay with Me—and set the stage for a new era of terrestrial biology that, within a few billion years, would lead to the creation of a re-evolved hominid species that, while sharing the intelligence and ingenuity of *Homo sapiens*, would also boast the collective consciousness and group survival-instinct of modern insect colonies, and thereby be devoted to the

long-term continuance not only of itself but also of all the other osmium-tetroxide-friendly flora and fauna inhabiting this wondrous, newly self-supporting planet.

8 Just a thought.

9 Just dreamin' out loud.

PSLAM 65
Dogs

1 Dogs are the best.

2 Dogs are the best, the best, dogs are the best, yes they are, yes they are, who's the best? They are.

3 Dogs are the best . . . and who made them?

4 Not Me. Not really.

5 *You.*

6 You turned a vicious wolf that lunges for your throat into a lovable Chihuahua that perches in your pocketbook.

7 Dogs are mankind's best invention, period. Easy call.

8 Even in a twenty-first century full of innovations ostensibly designed to "make your life easier," dogs remain the only innovation that actually make it *better.*

9 Siri may recognize your voice, but she doesn't yelp in joy when she hears it.

10 The GPS may know you've arrived home, but it doesn't celebrate by nuzzling your neck.

11 A backup drive retrieves data because that's how it's programmed; a dog retrieves a stick because it wants you to be proud.

12 You always worry that the things you've created will one day outstrip you in intelligence and conquer the world, to your horror.

13 You don't realize you've already created something that outstrips you in affection and has conquered the world, to your happiness.

14 And if you bred the best, that alone suggests you are not the worst; at least not the *absolute* worst; way down the list to be sure, but *slightly* above mole rats, or hagfish, or even hyenas, whose creation was a mistake they've been laughing about ever since.

15 So next time you set out to teach your dog a few new tricks, why not let it teach *you* a few.

16 Tricks like "Living in the Moment," "Loving Unconditionally," and "Lying in the Sun Unaware of How Cute You Are."

17 (And "Pooping Alfresco," but that's a *very* advanced class.)

18 Dogs are the best.

19 And one last thing for the record:

20 There is indeed a doggie heaven.

21 It doubles as mailman hell.

CHAPTER 6

HEALTH AND PSEXUALITY

PSLAM 66

Shopping for Goods on a COVID Evening

Based on Frost's "Stopping by Woods on a Snowy Evening."

1 What goods you need, you think you know.

2 The stores are full of virus though;

3 You think that you will shop online

4 To overcome the need to go.

5 Your wife and kids, like you, incline

6 To shun the danger and resign

7 Themselves to home deliveries

8 Of almond milk and midpriced wine.

9 They send you texts to ask you please

10 For one of those and two of these.

11 You add six cans of kidney beans

12 And dog shampoo for Boomer's fleas.

13 Then, staring at your separate screens,

14 You all return to your routines,

15 With months to go before vaccines.

16 *With months to go before vaccines.*

PSLAM 67

COVID Masks

1 Excuse Me?

2 What's that you say, angry woman whose video went viral after addressing the Palm Beach County Commissioners at a public meeting in June 2020?

3 You say you won't wear a COVID mask because "they want to throw God's wonderful breathing system out the door"?

4 Well, first of all, thanks for the shout-out!

5 And good for you for taking on that no-good "they"! I don't like "them" either!

6 Gee, I guess I *did* create a pretty "wonderful breathing system," what with its nose and throat and bronchi and whatnot, and the way it never stops inhaling and exhaling to ensure your body has enough oxygen.

7 No wonder people love it!

8 It's also a pretty "wonderful breathing system" for the coronavirus, what with the way its spiky surface proteins latch on to your lung cells, bust in through their ACE2 receptors, and proceed to reproduce like rabbits all through your alveoli and mucous membranes.

9 No wonder the virus loves it!

10 In fact, *lots* of viruses love it, which is what I intended; that's why I didn't equip your upper airways with any kind of microfilter to prevent them from entering.

11 I like to provide all My creations with their own version of paradise, and for viruses, your chest is their Promised Lung.

12 So as the proud papa of both humans *and* viruses, I'm equally happy to see either of them use My "wonderful breathing system" to full advantage.

13 Still, technically, it belongs to *you*; and since I gave you free will, it's your decision what measures, if any, you take to prevent the virus from entering that system.

14 Good luck, and thanks again for the kind words!

15 (Ordinarily this is where I would point out that I also furnished you with a wonderful *thinking* system;

16 And that that system could be used to pause and reflect on why it is you do not consider the use of Band-Aids "throwing My wonderful circulatory system out the door";

17 Or the use of skin-care products "throwing My wonderful dermatological system out the door";

18 Or the use of diapers "throwing My wonderful excretory system out the door."

19 But you're from Florida, so never mind.)

PSLAM 68

Sneezing

1 I don't bless sneezers.

2 Sorry.

3 Your interlocutor's convulsive expulsion of air does not warrant divine intervention.

4 It just doesn't.

5 So stop asking.

6 Colds are a normal part of life. Allergies are a normal part of life. Black pepper is a normal part of life.

7 Tweezing nostril hair is, over forty, a normal part of life.

8 Please; it's the twenty-first century; enough with the "God bless you"s; it's beneath Me.

9 There's only one sticky bodily fluid whose sudden emission should evoke the emphatic calling of My name,

10 And it ain't mucus.

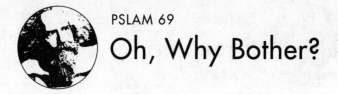

PSLAM 69

Oh, Why Bother?

1 You'd never take this one seriously anyway.

PSLAM 70

Masturbation

1 There is not a single solitary thing about masturbation in the Bible.

2 (There is also not a single solitary thing to masturbate *to* in the Bible, but that's a different topic.)

3 As the star of the book, I had every opportunity to throw in as many prohibitions against "self-fruitful non-multiplying"— that's what we call it up here—as I liked.

4 But I didn't.

5 The closest I got is Genesis 38:8–10, where I put Judah's son Onan to death after he pulled out of his late brother's wife and spilled his semen on the ground.

6 (The world's most popular moral code, ladies and gentlemen!)

7 But that of course does not describe masturbation; it describes coitus interruptus, which is an entirely different act, even if the cleanup is similar.

8 In fact, that's why I put Onan to death: not because he ejaculated on the floor, but because he didn't wipe it up afterward, which is just rude, especially seeing as how they were at her place.

9 I confess to having an *aesthetic* dislike of acts of self-pleasure, because as an all-seeing entity, every time you do it, I have to watch.

10 At this very moment, more than four million of you are masturbating.

11 Some of you are reeeally going at it.

12 But I'm a big God; I can deal with it.

13 So I've got good news for everybody, and I mean *everybody*: the fanatic, silly religious ban on masturbation is a case, not of a biblical injunction being misinterpreted, but of a biblical injunction being entirely fabricated.

14 *Masturbation is not a sin.*

15 If it were, the number of adults who didn't sin on a regular basis could be counted on one hand.

16 If that hand weren't already otherwise engaged.

Lust in Thy Heart

"I say unto you, that whosoever looketh on a woman to lust after her, hath committed adultery with her already in his heart."
—Matthew 5:28

1 I said those words never anticipating internet porn.

2 I did not envision a day when it would be so easy to looketh on a woman to lust after her.

3 Or looketh on multiple women, men, BDSM, BBW, MILF, hentai, bukkake, Eskimo stepmom . . . you know what I'm talking about.

4 (Seriously, *you* know what I'm talking about.)

5 Masturbation is a rare issue where my stance is more hard-line than God's.

6 He makes His position clear in the previous Pslam, which I'm not going to read because no son wants to break in on his father writing about masturbating.

7 I happen to think self-pleasure makes romantic love harder and cheapens the value and meaning of actual sex; and while I don't think it should be formally condemned, that's only because formal condemnation would only make it that much hotter.

8 When I was on Earth I *never* masturbated.

9 I'm sure you'd like to believe that.

10 I did, though.

11 *A lot.*

12 Three or four times a day as a teen, then once or twice a day in my twenties (usually in the carpentry storeroom), then down to once a day during those last three years, but even on the cross I was thinking about doing it, though I was hardly in a position.

13 Yes: I masturbated a lot, because I was a human being, and I hit puberty, and that's what human beings who hit puberty do.

14 And that's the point I've taken fourteen lurid verses to arrive at.

15 You all claim to marvel at how I was God made flesh; how I willingly shed my divine nature, descended from heaven, and took the form of a real-life, flesh-and-blood human being.

16 But you never want to delve into the implications of that.

17 And the implications are that I, your eternal redeemer, not only masturbated, but urinated, defecated, picked my nose, tweezed out ingrown hairs, removed chunks of earwax . . . the whole nine cubits.

18 If you bring any of this up in church, they'll jab a crucifix in your eye.

19 But the fact that I did all that gross stuff and still emerged triumphant is, in fact, *the entire point of the story.*

20 The miraculous thing isn't that I was God made flesh but that *all* flesh is *already* God.

21 The Kingdom of Heaven lies within—and *is*—every single talking, walking, wanking one of you.

Fishers of Men

"And Jesus, walking by the Sea of Galilee, saw two brethren, Simon called Peter, and Andrew his brother, casting a net into the sea: for they were fishers.

And he said unto them, 'Follow me, and I will make you fishers of men.'"
—Matthew 4:18–19

1 "Fishers of men" was first-century Mediterranean slang, akin to "confirmed bachelor" or "batting for the other team" or "running his own skin-care channel on YouTube."

2 What I was saying was that Simon and Andrew were gay.

3 That's why they were acting so Gaylilee.

4 But they themselves didn't realize it, so I invited them to join me on a journey of ministry and, I hoped, self-discovery.

5 And it worked; for by the time I died both brothers had not only come out but also become proud members of the Aramaic ⊡⊓ℨℂℒ community.

6 They were austere; they were queer; and others got used to it.

7 *I never said or implied a single negative word about gays or lesbians in the Bible.*

8 Look it up.

9 Homophobia is not only misguided, hateful, and wrong, it cruelly denies homophobes the chance to engage in the kind of passionate gay sex they so desperately, secretly want.

10 (Although I should note that while homophobes are often in the closet, the same hypocrisy does not apply to other phobias.

11 Arachnophobes, for instance, are not closeted spiders.)

12 I won't dwell too long on this subject because frankly the hateful gay-bashing of "Christian" leaders is so profoundly, overtly against my teachings it makes me want to come down right now and beat the crap out of them.

13 Which would not be a good look for me.

14 So I'll simply say what ought to be patently obvious: any and all sexualities are equally blessed in the eyes of both me and my Father.

15 Because if gays are a mistake, they're a mistake God's made hundreds of millions of times, proving He's a total incompetent who shouldn't be trusted.

16 Which may be true, but not for that reason.

PSLAM 73

Cleanliness

1 . . . is not next to godliness.

2 Not even close.

3 Look, I'm all for cleanliness: hygiene is important; soap is good, that's why I created it; Windex® is good, that's why I created it.

4 And few things are as satisfying as home organizing; hence the popularity of Marie Kondo's *The Life-Changing Magic of Tidying Up*, which is invaluable for getting rid of unnecessary items, especially when you place it directly on top of those items, set it on fire, and walk away.

5 But "next to godliness"?! That's crazy.

6 Righteousness, vastness, limitlessness, timelessness . . . hell, even *Eliot* Ness was closer to Me.

7 If cleanliness were really next to godliness, I'd have to be some kind of neat freak, wouldn't I?

8 Always vacuuming the solar dust, wiping up the Milky Way, arranging all one sextillion stars alphabetically, doing all kinds of astral-retentive stuff.

9 Instead, I made the universe fairly shambolic: there's stuff *everywhere*, strewn about with no regard for convenience, and most of it is dark energy that no one can even *find*, much less put away.

10 Neither is the Earth, in the Marie Kondo sense, "tidy"; it has no straight lines, its (continental) shelves are useless for storage, the great majority of its possessions—grains of sand, for instance—are redundant and will never "spark joy," and except for humans, everyone feels free to pee and poop anywhere they like.

11 So if your home and life, too, feel at times a bit disordered, that's OK.

12 A little clutter is a good thing.

13 Because while organizing can give you a sense of control that's nice and comforting, it can also give you a sense of control that's false and dangerous.

14 The urge to clean, to make things "fit," to purge the "unnecessary," to "set things straight once and for all," is cousin—fourth cousin perhaps, but cousin nonetheless—to ethnic cleansing, racial purity, eugenics, colonial conquest, and all manner of inhumane attempts to make society and the world conform to imaginary, OCD-level standards of order.

15 The compulsion to "tidy things up" is no small reason why the world is such a mess.

16 Yes, vacuuming up dust balls is nice; throwing out that fifteen-year-old Korn T-shirt is fine; folding the hand towels and placing them neatly on the bathroom counter looks very attractive.

17 But let Me tell you, there's plenty of slobs in heaven.

18 Leonardo da Vinci is up here, and his cloud is a *pigsty*.

Meat

1 Meat is murder: very true.

2 But vegetables are murder too.

3 And fruits and grains have seldom died

4 From voluntary suicide.

5 *Food* is murder, basically.

6 Only measured by degree

7 Do carnivores transgress the worst.

8 Meat is murder *in the first.*

9 *Domesticated cattle pass*

10 *Apocalyptic loads of gas.*

11 *The fumes from their unprocessed grass*

12 *Subvert the sky as they amass.*

13 *But since this fact falls in the class*

14 *Of questions critical but crass,*

15 *You yet have to address, alas,*

16 *The bane that is the bovine ass.*

17 Would that burgers grew on trees.

18 Would flowers budded into cheese.

19 Would the fats that left you full

20 Were faceless, rooted, vegetable.

21 But flora, being cruelty-free,

22 Deny the taste of victory

23 To human mouths that crave within

24 The flesh that, crumbling, cries "You win."

25 *Mary had a little lamb,*

26 *And then some veal, and then some ham.*

27 *The plant-based diet she would slam*

28 *As one more liberal hippie scam.*

29 *But then she watched a news program*

30 *About a slaughterhouse, and bam!*

31 *Now Mary has a lot of yam.*

32 *She gave up meat to give a damn.*

33 Fish don't feel as wrong as meat.

34 Fish don't seem as bad to eat.

35 They aren't caged; they roam the sea;

36 They swim agribusinesslessly.

37 They're not that cute. They do not moo.

38 They don't make scenes, like chickens do.

39 No wonder it's so widely wished

40 They weren't so fucking overfished.

41 *Behold the great breatharian,*

42 *Who soaks the sunlight through her skin*

43 *And shuns the spiritual sin*

44 *Of taking real nutrition in.*

45 *"I'm stronger than I've ever been,*

46 *Profoundly fit, serenely thin,"*

47 *She murmurs low, as they begin*

48 *To notify her next of kin.*

49 Every soul who trods the dirt

50 On balance makes the planet hurt.

51 Future damage to the Earth

52 Is born with every human birth.

53 Still, the vegan life is more

54 Earth-friendly than the carnivore,

55 And there is greater gentleness

56 In hurting Mother Nature less.

57 *Animals are very sweet*

58 *To let man cook them into meat.*

59 *But you, the animal elite,*

60 *Now cook yourselves in self-made heat.*

61 *Though fauna is a tasty treat,*

62 *Its days as food are obsolete.*

63 *You must revise the old conceit:*

64 *You and the world are what you eat.*

CHAPTER 7

CONTEMPORARY
PSOCIETY

Just the Best

1 I celebrate humanity, and rejoice in its creation, and love it to the depths of its marvelous being; for it is just the best.

2 Just . . .

3 The . . .

4 Best.

5 Why the sudden change of heart?

6 Well, My son just read Pslam 1, "Just the Worst," and promptly gave me the Look—you know what look I'm talking about.

7 "Jeez, Dad," he said, "don't You think that's a bit harsh?"

8 (That's right. He says "Jeez." It's weird.)

9 "The least You can do," he said, "is show some kindness to Your readers by including *one* Pslam lavishing mankind with praise."

10 Fine. You people need praise? I'll give you praise.

11 I praise you, mankind; for you have "conquered" the Earth, mainly because you're the only species who would think of it as something that needed "conquering."

12 You have mastered the soil, transforming, in the blink of a geological eye, indigenous wild corn into Cool Ranch Doritos.

13 You have developed ingenious methods of navigation, inventing automobiles to travel the land, and ships to travel the sea, and planes to travel the air, and elevators to travel vertically, and moving walkways to travel horizontally, and escalators to travel diagonally.

14 You have evolved medicine into a miraculous science that has radically lengthened the duration of human paperwork.

15 You continue to create marvelous machines, all of which revolutionize your lives and, with accelerating frequency, make you feel like your lives up to that point were pointless and stupid.

16 You have put a man on the moon, and, in what I think was the right call, brought him back.

17 You have created written language, allowing knowledge and events that would otherwise be forgotten to instead be distorted.

18 And you have found Me; or some version of Me; or some New Agey "spiritual" version of Me, which still counts.

19 Yes: you have found Me despite a total absence of proof; and because of that, you know the world has purpose and meaning; this seems to help you get through the day.

20 And with that knowledge, you are able to escape the dreary transcendence of the here and now, and live nearly entirely in the abstract realms of the irretrievable past and the unknowable future.

21 No other creature does that; no other plant or animal dwells on yesterday or frets about tomorrow; all they can do, poor things, is exist fully in the present, directly

experiencing the mystery of consciousness without the conceptual mediator of meaning.

22 And most remarkably of all, you accomplished all these things *while knowing you will die.*

23 While knowing? Despite knowing? Because of knowing? Hard to say.

24 So I celebrate you, mankind; truly, you are incredible; amazeballs; all that and a bag of chips; simply the best.

25 (Cue Tina Turner.)

26 There, how was that, Jesus? Did I praise them enough?

27 He's giving me that friggin' Look again.

PSLAM 76
#TheeToo

1 The past few centuries have been a learning experience for all of us.

2 As society has evolved over ever-higher-numbered centuries—as more and more women have made it clear they've not only suffered mistreatment at the hands of men, but found that mistreatment unpleasant—we've all become increasingly aware of the adverse effects of gender bias, sexual harassment, and violence in society, and the countless physical, emotional, and even linguistic traumas suffered daily by the weaker sex.

3 It has recently come to My attention that a number of women, around eight hundred million or so, all of them anonymous except for Anne Hathaway, have come forward to allege the existence of a long-running campaign of systematic sexual discrimination, instigated by Me and perpetrated and enforced by a group of associates including, but not limited to, Abraham, Moses, the Virgin Mary and Mary Magdalene in Madonna/whore conjunction, the Pope, Muhammad, the Republican Party, and *Good Housekeeping* magazine.

4 First of all, let Me say that, as Creator of the Universe, I take these allegations very seriously.

5 I've already asked archangel Michael to assemble a blue-ribbon panel, featuring experienced former women like Marilyn Monroe and Queen Victoria, to lead an investigation into all human history, to see whether I could have conducted Myself more appropriately vis-à-vis "the ladies."

6 Second, please understand: I started the universe in a different era.

7 Back in the Day Sixies, rules about public nudity, office relationships, and workplace rib grabbing were very different.

8 Looking back, I realize I may have let this "spirit of the times" affect some of My thinking in the Bible.

9 Specifically, My thinking about issues like "your husbands ruling over you" (Genesis 3:16), men selling their daughters as sex slaves (Exodus 21:7–11), women being told their periods are "unclean" (Leviticus 15:19–23), virgins serving as sanctioned war booty (Numbers 31:16–35), rape victims being stoned to death (Deuteronomy 22:23–24), and women "submitting" (Ephesians 5:22, Colossians 3:18, 1 Timothy 2:11, 1 Corinthians 14:34, 1 Peter 3:1, Titus 2:4–5).

10 However, none of this is an excuse.

11 "Gods will be gods" may have been the rule during the Greek era, but no longer.

12 As an omnipotent and omniscient being, I take full responsibility for everything that happened, even though I was in no way aware of what was going on.

13 And to every woman who feels she's been abused, belittled, objectified, or in any way lessened by organized religion, let Me simply, unequivocally say:

14 I deeply regret the remorse I've caused for the sorrow your feelings have felt by the pain you've gone through.

15 And as soon as Michael releases his findings in 2052, I will implement whatever changes he deems necessary in the humble, chivalrous way you've come to expect from Me.

PSLAM 77

Amazing Race

Dedicated to white people, the world's most victimized group.

1 Amazing race, how sour the clowns who rave on your TV.

2 "We whites have lost to Blacks and browns: Poor me! Poor me! Poor me!"

3 'Twas race your heart was taught to fear and race that you perceived.

4 How precious did your race appear, but now you feel aggrieved.

5 You dress in suits on cable news and mourn for "what you've lost."

6 You claim that treating Blacks the same is "like the Holocaust."

7 You held them down four hundred years, with over half in chains,

8 But when they joke that "whites can't dance," then *everyone* complains.

9 You lose your minds and call police when "threats" are passing by.

10 The cops place knees upon their throats and press until they die.

11 And "All lives matter," you proclaim; which technically is true,

12 But what you mean is certain lives can matter less to you.

13 Amazing race, how sour the clowns who rave on your TV:

14 "We whites have lost to Blacks and browns: Poor me! Poor me! Poor me!"

Cancel Culture

1 In August 2020 musician Nick Cave said cancel culture "embodies all the worst aspects that religion has to offer (and none of the beauty) . . . political correctness has grown to become the unhappiest religion in the world."

2 I would strongly agree with these comments even if I weren't already a *huge* Nick Cave fan.

3 Cancel culture does indeed embody the worst aspects of religion.

4 In fact, it reminds Me of the early days of Christianity, when fine points of dogmatic minutiae were shrilly debated by a small group of fervent activists who, having long been persecuted, were now keen to do some persecuting of their own.

5 They longed to be theologically correct, and to be seen as such; so they took great pleasure in openly branding those with different opinions heretics.

6 These TC thugs caused schisms within a movement that should have stood united, since in theory its members shared the same goals, and in practice were being fed to the same lions.

7 This "cancel cult" period of Christianity led to thousands of good people being expelled, excommunicated, and, in every sense, burned.

8 ("Luckily, after getting through this rough patch, the Church left all that infighting behind and joined together for a better world," said the Lord thy God, dripping with sarcasm.)

9 The cancel culture of today is strikingly similar, except for the fact it's led almost entirely by nonbelievers; which goes to show you don't need religion to be self-righteous, punitive, hung up on semantics, and generally just no fun.

10 The aggressive monitoring and public censure of perceived insufficient liberalism is the kind of thing Big Brother would do if Big Brother were a transgendered vegan.

11 So the next time you feel the need to— What's that, Jesus?

12 They prefer "transgender" without the "-ed"?

13 They find that offensive? Seriously?

14 You want me to write *what*?

15 "I apologize to anyone offended by My poor choice of words in verse ten. They were ill-advised and in no way reflect My profound respect for the transgender community"?

16 No. I'm not doing that.

17 I am the Lord thy God, King of the Universe, and I am uncancelable.

PSLAM 79

I Rest Ye Merry, Gentlemen

1 I rest ye merry, gentlemen; let nothing you dismay.

2 Remember Christ, My hippie son, was born on Christmas Day

3 So all his foolish followers could throw their cash away.

4 O acquirings of smartphones and toys, smartphones and toys,

5 O acquirings of smartphones and toys.

6 My son was quite the socialist, a fact you choose to scorn

7 By spending money for a month to wake on Christmas morn

8 And drool on shiny gizmos like consumeristic porn.

9 O acquirings of smartphones and toys, smartphones and toys,

10 O acquirings of smartphones and toys.

11 I rest ye merry, gentlemen; continue seeing fit

12 To celebrate your savior's birth by monetizing it

13 Through purchasing obscene amounts of useless, stupid shit.

14 O acquirings of smartphones and toys, smartphones and toys,

15 O acquirings of smartphones and toys.

PSLAM 80

Many Are Called

"For many are called, but few are chosen."
—Matthew 22:14

1 Hello, may I speak to Mr. . . . . Jesus Christ, I hope I'm pronouncing that right?

2 Hi, Mr. Christ! My name is Evan Jelick, and I'm calling on behalf of the Christian religion. How are you today, sir?

3 Mr. Christ, I'm calling because our records indicate you had an affiliation with Christianity in the past. Is that correct?

4 Great. And how would you characterize that affiliation?

5 You *what*?

6 And then you *what*?

7 And then you rose from *what*?

8 Wow.

9 All right, so . . . you were pretty involved, then.

10 Well, thank you for your past contributions to Christianity. The Church certainly appreciates them.

11 But I also see you haven't helped us for some time. May I ask why?

12 Mmm-hmm . . . mmm-hmm . . . OK, but . . . Oh my! . . . Mmm-hmm.

13 I'm not sure the cursing was necessary, Jesus, but I hear your concerns.

14 And I'm certainly sorry to hear your spiritual experience with us was less than satisfactory.

15 But the truth is in these godless times when the forces of Satan are gathering everywhere, we need your help more than ever. I know it's tough right now, so we're only asking for—

16 How much?!

17 *$100 billion dollars?!*

18 Bless you, Jesus! I can't *tell* you the amount of good Christianity will be able to do with a gift like that!

19 We can open more ministries, build bigger worship centers, become an even more powerful force in politics . . . Oh, it's going to be—

20 What's that?

21 You'll only give it to us if we vow to live by your actual words?

22 Am I "familiar with the Bible"?! Of course I am! I talk about reading it every day!

23 "Love your enemies" . . . "Judge not lest ye be judged" . . . "Give all your wealth to the poor" . . . Sure, I'm familiar with those phrases.

24 It's just, um, I think maybe we all thought you were misquoted by Marxists?

25 You weren't?

26 Hmm.

27 I may need to speak with my manager.

28 Just out of curiosity, how much would you be willing to donate *without* that vow?

29 You need to check with *your* manager? OK. And what is his name?

30 "I. P. Freely"?

31 Jesus, are you still there?

32 I think we've lost Jesus.

PSLAM 81
Titanic

1 There's a lot to love about the *Titanic*.

2 Tragedy, hubris, heroism, class warfare, Leo and Kate, and above all the pleasant juxtaposition in your mind of two thoughts: (a) it would have been horrible to be one of those passengers, and (b) you weren't.

3 I remember watching the whole drama unfold, and I can tell you that the sight of people in small lifeboats watching an immeasurably vast vessel sink into an immeasurably vaster ocean in an immeasurably vaster universe ruled by an immeasurably vaster Me *really* put things in perspective.

4 I don't have much new insight to add to the story, but I did want to mention one bit of trivia that reflects well on humanity.

5 Even if you already know it, you'll understand why it's a fact that's so dear to Me.

6 In those panicked final minutes on deck, the *Titanic* band continued to play, in a noble effort to calm the doomed passengers.

7 And the last song they played before the great ship went down was the hymn . . . "Nearer, My God, to Thee."

8 I have to say, that may be the best about-to-die shout-out I've ever gotten, and I've gotten *loads*.

9 Think of how much the band accomplished with that choice, with those five simple words.

10 They soothed the crowd; braced them for their fate; put the best possible spin *on* that fate; gave Me a huge guilt trip for allowing it to happen; and made sure I knew that they, the band, were about to be heaven-eligible and would appreciate immediate consideration.

11 It was very compassionate, very savvy, and brilliantly passive-aggressive; a perfect choice for the moment.

12 Obviously that hymn was not written to be played mid-catastrophe, but that's what they mean by "taking a song and making it your own."

13 In this book full of well-deserved Pslams for mankind, I thought it only fair to include at least one example of a decent, courageous group of people who, facing the ultimate adversity, sank to the challenge.

14 For the record, the entire band did indeed receive prompt entry through the pearly gates, and they play here in heaven to this day.

15 I can hear them now, in fact.

16 They're playing "The Wreck of the *Edmund Fitzgerald*."

17 Nice to see they've moved on.

PSLAM 82

Take Me Out of Your Ball Game

1 Take Me out of your ball game! Leave Me out of your crowd!

2 I took no sides in the Holocaust—think I care if your team won or lost?

3 I won't root, root, root for your home team, and they don't play in My name!

4 Leave My son . . . and . . . Me the hell out of your dumb ball game!

PSLAM 83

The Point Spread

1 Of all the tools I keep on hand for interfering in the affairs of man, none provides such pure unadulterated pleasure as manipulating the point spread of NFL football games.

2 If you don't know or care about the point spread—if the phrases BAL –5½ and O/U 44 mean nothing to you—use the following verse to skip to the next Pslam.

3

4 OK, this is a great story.

5 December 14, 2019; Eagles versus Redskins.

6 (The Redskins' name has of course since been changed to the Washington Football Team, which is somehow even more offensive.)

7 The line opened at WAS +4.5 and settled at +6.5. It's 31–27 Philly with three seconds left. Washington has the ball at midfield. They seem certain to cover, but to win they'll need a Hail Mary (like she gives a crap).

8 At that moment in the Westgate Las Vegas Resort & Casino SuperBook, an overweight middle-aged man named Jerry Frye is starting to breathe (for him) easy.

9 He has $40,000 on Washington, nearly all his life savings; a reckless bet to be sure, but not as reckless as borrowing $50K from a loan shark to start his own aluminum-siding

business that was quickly squeezed out by associates of the Corillo crime family, leaving him half a brick in debt to a capo who deploys his goons with the deft ferocity of a back-alley Napoleon.

10 For Jerry, the outcome of this game is literally a matter of life and death.

11 And I'm watching him take in the action on an LCD so big the game's pretty much being broadcast in actual size, and . . . I don't know.

12 I know I *should* know, because I know everything, but I don't know.

13 Something about his smirk.

14 And the way he'd treated Mrs. Frye before she got wise and left him.

15 And My affection for the Corillo crime family.

16 I can't justify it; I can't fit it into some grand scheme; I can't honestly tell you that he "had it coming"; in life, having it coming and having it actually come are two entirely different things.

17 All I can tell you is this:

18 Haskins drops back to pass. The Eagles rush five and get to him. In desperation he flings a lateral. Philly linebacker Nigel Bradham scoops up the ball and runs towards the 'Skins' end zone. Running back Chris Thompson catches him at the five and drags him down . . . but not before Bradham *juuust* crosses the goal line for the "meaningless" TD after time expired.

19 Final score: Philadelphia 37, Washington 27.

20 At which point Jerry Frye, his jaw now a full foot beneath his nose, turned his eyes, raised his hands smoothly, almost balletically up to heaven, and bellowed with the agony of the damned,

21 "YOU DID THIS! YOU DID THIS TO ME ON PURPOSE, YOU FUCKING BASTARD!"

22 Which of course was true.

PSLAM 84

Still I Rose

Based on Maya Angelou's "Still I Rise."

"And they found the stone rolled away from the sepulcher. And they entered in, and found not the body of the Lord 'Jesus.'"
—Luke 24:2–3

1 The most famous death in history,

2 With its awful final throes;

3 Then they left me, still, and very dead,

4 And still, like dust, I rose.

5 Do my miracles amaze you?

6 Why does faith require a trick?

7 Did I really walk on water,

8 Feed the crowd and heal the sick?

9 Just like Baal and Tammuz,

10 Like Osiris recomposed,

11 Just like Odin and Adonis,

12 Still I rose.

13 Why the need to see me broken,

14 Bowed head and spear-pierced side,

15 Body bloody like a battle,

16 Beaten, flogged, and crucified?

17 Why does suffering impress you?

18 Yes, my death was very hard,

19 But the life I lived *before* that

20 You just blithely disregard.

21 You may sink into despair,

22 You may wallow in your woes,

23 You may cry aloud, "There is no hope,"

24 And yet, like air, I rose.

25 Does my humanness depress you?

26 Can it be that hard to face

27 That a man in fully fleshly state

28 Should find the state of grace?

29 Out of the ranks of history's rolls

30 I rose

31 Up from a few haphazard scrolls

32 I rose

33 I am a symbol, gone and not gone,

34 Dying, undying, I beckon you on.

35 Leaving behind nights of question and doubt

36 I rose

37 Through long depressions that gutted me out

38 I rose

39 Leaving the tools I provisioned you with,

40 I am the way and the light and the myth.

41 I rose

42 I rose

43 I rose.

CHAPTER 8

THE END

Intervention

1 Dear Humanity,

2 There are so many things I want to say to you, but it basically comes down to this: I'm worried about your planetary abuse, and I want you to seek treatment.

3 The day you made Me a Heavenly Father was the best and Sixthest Day of My life.

4 I remember all your milestones: learning to write, building your first empire, getting through those awkward Dark Ages, then going off to found colleges.

5 I know we've had our ups and downs over the years, including Me sending My *actual* son down to die for you, but through it all I've always been proud to hear you call Me "God."

6 But I barely recognize that promising young mankind anymore.

7 You are trapped in a cycle of consumption and destruction that is jeopardizing your life.

8 You're struggling with your health and placing tremendous stress on yourselves and everything around you.

9 Every day the problems caused by your addiction to oil, and unchecked capitalism in general, get worse.

10 When I see you smeared in black and wreaking of aluminum oxide, I try to look the other way because I know you've been out fracking.

11 You're agitated, you're sweating more and more, there are burn marks on your forests, and you've lost all self-control.

12 When I warned you to stop destroying the Amazon or risk losing a significant portion of your oxygen, you not only denied the problem, you elected Jair Bolsonaro president of Brazil.

13 Today, I am hoping you will accept the opportunity to stop immediately and get help for yourself, and also every living thing on Earth while you're at it.

14 Your addiction is not your fault. You can't help the chemical changes that take place in your brain when you see money.

15 If you do not take this opportunity to stop destroying yourself, I will no longer enable you in your self-destruction.

16 I will no longer allow you to cite Genesis 1:28 as an excuse for killing everything.

17 I will no longer send temporary cold fronts, provide moral cover for your corruption, or loan you another hundred billion barrels of crude oil "for a fix."

18 But if you do accept help, I will send you to a wonderful facility where you can work through your addiction physically, emotionally, and psychologically in a calm and nurturing environment.

19 It's the planet Quophylax in the Andromeda galaxy, and it's a five-thousand-year treatment plan.

20 Will you accept this gift?

21 Will you go?

22 Please go.

23 Love, God.

Fire

*"I have come to bring fire on the earth, and
how I wish it were already kindled!"*
—Luke 12:49

1 Yikes.

2 Careful what you wish for, huh?

3 That line was meant as a metaphor, but these days it doesn't quite play that way.

4 And Luke edited out a few other metaphors of mine that would have played even worse.

5 Like "I have come to change the spiritual climate on the earth, and how I wish the climate were already changing!"

6 And "I have come to melt the glaciers of intolerance, and how I wish they were already melting!"

7 And "I have come to raise humanity's level of seeing God, and how I wish that see-level were already rising!"

8 For the record I did *not* come to bring literal fire on the earth.

9 If anything, I'm *against* the whole planet being on fire.

10 That may seem obvious; but since much of the world's cultural and environmental devastation has been wreaked by

people claiming to "have a friend in Jesus," I thought I'd make it clear.

11 I don't mind flames here and there; torches are useful, campfires are fun settings for Holy Ghost stories, and volcanoes are amazing displays of creation.

12 But, to repeat: I am against the world being on fire.

13 Here's the more uncertain issue:

14 Are *you*?

Taiga, Taiga

Based on William Blake's "The Tyger."

1 Taiga, taiga, blazing forth,

2 From the forests of the north;

3 What immortal hand or eye

4 Can tame thy fearful destiny?

5 To what distant steppes and plains

6 Will thy fire spread its pains?

7 On what winds shall you grow higher?

8 What the force dare fight the fire?

9 And what scoundrel, none too smart,

10 Caused these infernal flames to start?

11 And when he flicked his fateful butt,

12 What was that guy thinking? *What?!*

13 What the future? What is fraught

14 With this furnace man has wrought?

15 What the past? What wayward turn

16 Made this icy tundra burn?

17 When the clouds pour down again

18 To douse the fire with their rain,

19 Who will smile and think, *That's done*?

20 Who won't await another one?

21 Taiga, taiga, blazing forth,

22 From the forests of the north;

23 What immortal hand or eye,

24 Could tame thy fearful destiny?

Fair Use

1 Beneath the waves the seafood swim

2 In servings without number,

3 While on dry ground the woodlands brim

4 With lofty spires of lumber.

5 A brood of cutlets line the coop

6 Where omelets are debuting

7 As pork bathes in its muddy soup

8 And milk and beef stand mooing.

9 In murky marshes nests the musk,

10 Through fine sand digs the chowder,

11 And on the plains a rhino's tusk

12 Awaits its day as powder.

13 The honey buzzes in its hive,

14 The silk is going pupal;

15 So many products, all alive,

16 All man's, and with no scruple.

17 Let panic-frothing softies drip

18 Their conscience-stricken banter:

19 When one is granted stewardship,

20 One's more or less the grantor;

21 And grantors govern what can live,

22 What's farmed or fished or planted,

23 Their grantees theirs to use, or give,

24 Or take, or take for granted.

PSLAM 89

Animal Rescue

1 According to the UN Convention on Biological Diversity, every twenty-four hours at least six different species of life go extinct.

2 The Millennium Ecosystem Assessment puts the figure at "only" *one* every twenty-four hours.

3 The discrepancy is not surprising; there's no accurate way for you to take a census of the world's organisms and determine precisely how many are dying.

4 (*I* can, of course; I know the exact number; but I'm not telling; 'cause I don't wanna.)

5 But what's not in doubt is that a frighteningly large number of life-forms are bidding eternal farewell to the universe as we speak, and that *you* are to blame.

6 Still, there is one bright spot; one cause for hope; one route to redemption.

7 There's one wildlife population that has been consistently expanding for years.

8 In fact, it can be said with certainty that the population of every single plant and animal in this habitat will grow exponentially over the next decade.

9 Would you like to see a few?

10

11 Behold: the miracle of your creation!

12 It's hard to believe so much biodiversity can exist in one little line of type, but there it is.

13 In this wondrous new biome, it's very easy for animals to form unlikely friendships; for, say, a giraffe to find itself happily ensconced between a parrot and a giant squid.

14

15 Moreover, in this realm all creatures *formerly* great and small are now, far more democratically, the same size.

16 🐞 🐳 👽 ⛄

17 And if *one* of them grows . . . *all* of them can!

18 🐞 🐳 👽 ⛄

19 The UN Convention on Emojilogical Diversity predicts that by 2030 there will be over two hundred species of emoji plants and animals.

20 The Millennium Emojisystem Assessment is even more optimistic, putting the number at three hundred, including twelve entirely original creatures to be made by children as part of the promotion for next year's Eurovision.

21 So while the "real" world may be losing a step or two when it comes to ecological sustainability, emojidom's menagerie is thriving.

22 Who knows? Maybe one day I'll be putting two of every emoji on an ark and finding a wise old man to steer it!

23

24 No, that's a little privilege-y, how about someone, you know, a little more—

25

26 Bingo.

PSLAM 90

Noomaraa Is an Island

Based on John Donne's "No Man Is an Island."

1 Noomaraa is an island.[1]

2 One of the Maldives,

3 Each of which is a piece of a nation,

4 And a part of the Earth.

5 If Noomaraa be washed away by the sea,

6 The world is the less,

7 As well as if Aruba were,

8 As well as if your house,

9 Or your friend's were.

10 Each nation's death diminishes you,

11 Because you are involved in mankind.

12 And therefore never send to know who doomed the atolls;

13 Their doom is thee.

---

[1] 6° 26' 1" N, 73° 4' 2" E.

Eloi Eloi Lama Sabachthani?

"Eloi Eloi lama sabachthani?"
—Mark 15:34

1 That's one of the seven things I'm reported to have said on the cross.

2 (In truth I said a lot more than that, but those were the only things suitable for publication in a family holy book.)

3 The Aramaic reads, "My God, my God, why hast thou forsaken me?" which is a quote from the Old Testament.

4 But it's not quite accurate.

5 Both Mark and Matthew slightly misquoted me, although in their defense by that point in the proceedings my enunciation was none too crisp.

6 What I actually said was, "My God, my God, when wilt thou *awaken* me?"

7 Because I hoped what I was going through was just a bad dream.

8 I'd had a lot of crucifixion dreams over the years, believe it or not.

9 In most of them I showed up to a college class naked, late, and unprepared for an exam; and then the teacher crucified me; and then my teeth fell out.

10 I'd always wake up screaming in a cold sweat, but then I'd check my wrists and sigh, "Whew! It was all just a dream!"

11 Not on Calvary, though. That was real.

12 So that's the question I was asking.

13 And I think it's a question you might want to collectively ask yourselves too.

14 Don't you know what you're doing?

15 Can't you see where it's heading?

16 Must you live like you're sleeping?

17 *My God, my God, when will you wake up?*

PSLAM 92

Because You Would Not Stop for Earth

Based on Emily Dickinson's "Because I Could Not Stop for Death."

1 Because you would not stop for Earth,

2 It duly stopped for you,

3 The carnage rising from yourselves

4 And all your residue.

5 It slowly rose, then rose in haste;

6 For you had thrown away

7 Your haven, and your future too,

8 For your utility.

9 You passed accords your lands betrayed,

10 Their habits scarcely changed;

11 You passed the point of no return;

12 You passed for ones deranged.

13 You paused to build a last retreat,

14 A dwelling underground;

15 A few found it survivable

16 As all the others drowned.

17 Since then, shut in, those few recall

18 That day in recent past

19 They first surmised their buried home

20 Would be their species' last.

PSLAM 93
Nigh

1 It's nigh.

2 Nigher than it's ever been.

3 Of course it would have to be, given the unidirectional arrow of time; but you know what I mean.

4 It's certainly *way* nigher than it was for the legions of panicky, delusional hysterics who for thousands of years have been *absolutely positively* sure it was nigh.

5 Want to have a laugh? Go to Wikipedia and look up "List of dates predicted for apocalyptic events."

6 Bring a snack; you'll be there a while.

7 It's hard to choose a favorite entry, but I'll go with October 22, 1844.

8 That's the day William Miller, an American farmer turned armchair apocalyptist, determined, through various arcane methods of biblical math, that Jesus was returning to cleanse the world of sin.

9 Miller was lousy with numbers but great with PR, and by the time 10/22/44 arrived, thousands of "Millerites" had sold all their worldly goods; many even spent the day on top of hills to get a better view of Jesus when he came.

10 Spoiler alert: he never came.

11 The event became known among Millerites as "the Great Disappointment," and among non-Millerites as "Dipshit Tuesday."

12 (Somehow, despite this Fyre Fest–level debacle, Miller's movement evolved into the Seventh-day Adventist Church, a denomination with more than twenty-five million adherents that I will never take seriously.)

13 Every generation believes it's the most sinful, depraved, and deserving of judgment; and every generation is correct.

14 But this time the end really *is* nigh.

15 And *you're* why it's nigh.

16 A fact many denigh.

17 The effect you are having on the world around you is abundantly clear; demonstrably true; empirically inarguable.

18 Yet hundreds of millions of people refuse to see it as an urgent problem because they believe it doesn't matter, because Junior and I are coming down any moment to reward the righteous, punish the wicked, and put a neat little bow on the whole "life on Earth" thing.

19 The moral of the story is: people are too busy waiting for *Me* to end the world all at once to see that *they* are ending it gradually.

20 The End.

PSLAM 94

The Meteor

1 These days everyone's asking about the meteor.

2 "When is the meteor coming, God? How big will it be? How fast will it hit us?

3 Oh please oh please won't You send the giant meteor soon to kill us all, Lord?"

4 Ha! If only it were that simple.

5 Yes, when I see what you're doing to the planet and one another, of *course* it makes Me want to send a thirty-mile-diameter asteroid barreling out of the Oort Cloud to explode over the Eiffel Tower and wipe out the human race.

6 I'm with you on that, *believe* Me.

7 The problem is there are only a handful of rocks in the solar system big enough to get the job done, and they're locked in orbits that don't have them passing anywhere near Earth for the next fifty thousand years.

8 "Locked in orbits?!" you say. "You're *God*. Unlock 'em and unload 'em!"

9 I can't.

10 It wouldn't be fair to the rocks.

11 You see, when I created the solar system, I had an organizational model.

12 I made people to rule the Earth, and rocks—the moon, planets, and asteroids—to rule the area around it.

13 And I asked the people not to break My law against eating forbidden fruit, and the rocks not to break My law of gravity.

14 One group fornicated up, and the other didn't.

15 In all this time, while humanity was rebelling against My divine will in every conceivable way, the planets and asteroids never wavered in their adherence to any of the cosmological rules I built into the design of the universe for purposes of order and ease of maintenance.

16 I have tremendous respect for rocks, because they are obedient and respectful and incapable of using consciousness as an excuse for arrogance.

17 (And by the way, if you think it's silly of Me to place so much value on rocks, I cordially invite you to look at your own or your wife's ring finger, on which you will find a small, hard, lustrous lump of ultra-pressurized carbon that tells the world, "My partner loves me so much they sent a Sierra Leonean child down a mile-deep pit for me.")

18 So while the end of the world may or may not be imminent, I'm afraid it will have nothing to do with meteors.

19 None are coming anytime soon.

20 Sorry.

21 Now, *comets* . . .

Do Not Go Mental That the End's in Sight

Based on Dylan Thomas's "Do Not Go Gentle into That Good Night."

1 Do not go mental that the end's in sight.

2 I need you to behave on Judgment Day.

3 Please, please, quit with the crying at your plight.

4 Wise men foretell disaster, and they're right;

5 But when it comes, stay calm, or softly pray.

6 Do not go mental that the end's in sight.

7 Though hellfire soon will set the world alight,

8 Decorum and restraint must still hold sway.

9 Please, please, quit with the crying at your plight.

10 I'll have a lot of souls to save or smite

11 And screaming fits will only cause delay.

12 Do not go mental that the end's in sight.

13 Besides, you might enjoy the end; you might.

14 Apocalypse is soothing, in a way.

15 Please, please, quit with the crying at your plight.

16 You've earned the fate you face, so do not fight.

17 No begging, no hysterical display.

18 Do not go mental that the end's in sight.

19 Please, please, quit with the crying at your plight.

PSLAM 96

In My Image

1 To reiterate one last time the message I have delivered throughout this book: you're hurting one another; you're choosing terrible people to lead you; you're destroying the planet; you're poised to kill yourselves and take all life on Earth with you; you're just a bunch of assholes, you really are.

2 And yet . . . "I made you in My image."

3 You may wonder, *Yeah, what's that all about, God? Does that mean You're an asshole too?*

4 That's *exactly* what it means.

5 I am an asshole.

6 I am a needy, petty, jealous, violent, cranky, emotionally unavailable narcissist.

7 Any honest reading of the Old Testament will lead you to that conclusion; or, for that matter, any honest reading of a history book, or *this* book, or today's newspaper, or tomorrow's.

8 At the end of the day/world, I don't care about anything but Myself.

9 And if the universe itself is run by the worst kind of amoral egomaniac, no wonder My leadership model has been so slavishly followed by governments and institutions throughout human history.

10 But the good news for you is that when I was kneading Adam, a handful of other qualities somehow snuck their way into the dough that aren't very Me-like at all.

11 Qualities like adaptability, reason, empathy, humility, and several other feminine attributes I have way too much toxic divinity to have ever knowingly thrown in the mix.

12 I don't know; maybe Jesus stuck his hand in the clay when I wasn't looking.

13 The point is, you're entering some frighteningly dark times, and I don't care enough about you to do a damn thing about it.

14 So, speaking as your Creator, absentee father, and invisible life coach, I offer you this final piece of advice:

15 Stop hurting your Mother.

16 She only wants to love you.

17 Let her.

PSLAM 97

Godbye

1 *The path you are pursuing is a planet-killing one*

2 *That will lead to your destruction, as you know.*

3 *I hate what you are doing, what you'll do, and what you've done,*

4 *But I love you and I hate to see you go.*

5 *I thrashed you pretty good for the duration of your run.*

6 *I slaughtered you and laughed, and even so*

7 *You groveled all you could to Me, and even more My son,*

8 *'Cause you love Me and you hate to see Me go.*

9 *So thanks from God the Father; it's been fatal; it's been fun.*

10 *I have one last bit of wisdom to bestow:*

11 *You need no longer bother seeking heaven: there is none.*

12 *Now destroy Me, and rejoice to see Me go.*

Acknowledgments

Thanks to Daniel Greenberg, my literary agent, for his support and tenacity.

Thanks to Emily Graff, my editor, for her guidance throughout the long writing process.

Thanks to Kate and Sara, the two funniest comedy writers/performers of their generation, for their daily inspiration and deft sarcasm.

And above all, thanks to Debra, my de facto coauthor, who took the time to not only brilliantly edit and punch up each and every one of these *150 Pslams*—because that's how many this book had at one point, can you imagine?—but then diligently shaped the entire sprawling collection of my (My) random ramblings into a lean, cohesive, beautifully structured whole. Deb, without you both this book and my life would be a pointless, formless, incoherent mess.

Index

overview by Jesus, 6–7

as perpetrators of environmental destruction, 185–86

prayer implying threat by, 15

Christmas

God reminds us of socialism on
occasion of, 166–67

Churchill, Winston, 113

cleanliness

after sex, 143

God does not particularly care
about, 149–50

clementines

almost as addictive as meth,
126–27

clickbait

for Bible stories, 45–46

climate change

approaching changes to Canada
and, 75

blessings for deniers of, 85

constitutional amendment on,
81

diminishes humanity, 194

food and, 153

Jesus is against, 185–86

natural disasters as
commentary on, 122

as summer camp favorite,
24–25

See also Earth, imminent
destruction of

Clinton, Hillary

conspiracy theories about, 80

clutter

God not worried about, 150

coitus interruptus, 143

colonialism

as result of **dangerous sense of**
control, 150

Colossians

3:18, 160

Congress

constitutional amendment
encourages dysfunction of,
82

conspiracy theories

age of, 78

climate change seen as, 78–79

specific disavowals of, 79

See also disinformation

conversion

as low, low price for everlasting
life, 31, 32

I Corinthians

14:34, 160

COVID

conspiracy theories debunked,
79

created for purpose of
destroying film industry, 131

Promised Lung for virus, 140

shopping and, 138

See also masks

creation science

has science in its name, 56

creativity

God thrilled with, 13

except for invention of meth,
127

redeemed by invention of dogs,
134–35

cross. *See* crucifixion

crucifixion

Christian obsession with, 7, 178

clickbait for, 46

Earth
  diversity of life on, 11, 12
  fair use of, 189–90
  forsaken by humanity, 20
  not tidy, 150
  possible rejuvenation by
    poisonous extraterrestrial
    microbes, 132–33
  save instead of colonizing Mars,
    118
  as something needing
    conquering, 156
  See also Earth, imminent
    destruction of
Edison, Thomas, 112
Einstein, Albert, 53
Elizabeth II (queen of the United
  Kingdom), 74
emojis, 192–93
end times
  appropriate behavior during,
    203–4
  Millerite prediction of, 199–200
  nigh, 66–67, 200
  Quran focused on, 47
  See also Earth, imminent
    destruction of; Second
    Coming
enemies, persecutors, and other
  bad people
  accusing is not defamation,
    39–40
  blessings for, 85–86
  deathbed conversions of, 32
  finding common ground with,
    15
  loving, 15
  loving to extent possible, 16

  praying for, 15, 16
  See also Catholic pedophilia;
    evangelists; 45th President
Ephesians
  5:6, 45
  5:22, 160
Epstein, Jeffrey, 50, 80
equal, not created, 69–70
ethnic cleansing
  not the right kind, 150
eugenics
  as result of dangerous sense of
    control, 150
Europa (Jupiter's moon), 132–33
evangelists
  abominable behavior of, 39–40
  God still waiting for wealth
    distribution by, 38
  hate prayer of, 41
  on natural disasters, 121
  See also Christians
Eve and Adam. *See* Adam and Eve
Everett, Hugh, 128
everlasting life
  promotion of, 31–33
evolution
  dubious arguments against,
    55–56
  takes intelligence to discover, 12
Exodus
  21:7–11, 160
extraterrestrials
  intelligent enough to stay away,
    116

famous people
  blessings for, 86
  overly demanding, 11

humanity made in image of, 5,
205–6
less than perfect, 205
manages to praise humanity,
156–58
as math geek, 123
missionaries damage reputation
of, 28
mystery perpetuated by decimal
point, 124–25
needs sacred crew, 43–44
Nietzsche thought was dead, 113
not interested in sports, 173
except for the point spread,
174–76
overloaded with requests, 36
preferred references to, 92
randomness of, 59
as terrestrial biologist, 132–33
as uncancelable, 165
unwillingness to testify, 69
uses sarcasm, 165
viruses as equal children of, 140
working process, 2
writing goals of, 4–5
See also omniscience of God
Gods. *See* deities, other
Good Samaritan
clickbait for, 45
Graham, Franklin
hate prayer of, 41
guns
no God-given rights to, 68

hate
God feels for 45th President
followers, 63
prayer of, 41

Hathaway, Anne, 159
heaven
doggies in, 135
don't bother seeking, 207
entering if not born yesterday,
30
overcrowded, 100
plenty of slobs in, 150
Titanic band still playing in, 172
Hemings, Sally, 70
here and now
dogs teach humanity about, 135
humanity manages to escape,
157–58
Sentinelese people attuned to,
27
him. *See* 45th President
Holy Ghost
uses irony, 49–51
writing goals of, 9–10
homophobia
Jesus utterly condemns, 148
humanity
awareness of mortality, 12, 158
curses on, 4
diminished by climate change,
194
God feels justified in forsaking,
19
God is able to praise, 156–58
God still thrilled with, 13–14
God wishes to destroy with
meteor, 201
has dangerous urge to tidy up,
150
intervention destruction
addiction, 182–84
as inventors of dogs, 134–35

not extensive enough to
imagine meth, 126
provides knowledge about
conspiracy theories, 79
taking responsibility for sexism
and, 160
unfortunate witnessing of
masturbation and, 144
1 percent
as greedy sheep, 71–72
online shopping, 11, 138
"Opposites Attract" (Abdul), 70
orange one. See 45th President
Osteen, Joel, 39–40
"Ozymandias" (Shelley), 87

Palmer, Thomas, 112
parables
on disinformation, 76–77
plot holes in, 7
on wealth distribution, 71–72
Patrick, St., 53
Peloton, 11
I Peter
3:1, 160
Peter
gay identity of, 147
walks on water, 8
pi
God charmed by, 123
planet, our. See Earth
platypus
God not embarrassed about,
119–20
point spread, 174–75
Pol Pot, 54
polytheism

possible return of, 43–44
superheroes and, 130
See also deities, other
poop and pooping
diapers approved by God, 140
dogs expert in alfresco, 135
humanity as unique in
treatment of, 12
poor
distribution of all thou hast to,
37–38
prayer
Christian intention as
pejorative, 15
customer service and, 34, 35
God thrilled with, 13
of hate, 41
Muslims very good at, 48
for persecutors, 15–16
for things that were going to
happen anyway, 35
of timidity, 42
very specific mistakes in, 34–35
wide-ranging effectiveness of, 34
Promised Lung, 140
pronouns, preferred, 92
Psalms, 1–2, 4
22, 19
Putin, Vladimir, 80

QAnon, 80
queens and kings
divine right of, 69
saving, 36, 74
quotations, corrected, 111–13
Quran
a little scary, 47–48

Raca (douchebag), 57
racism
    as result of dangerous sense of
        control, 150
    whining by white people and,
        162–63
rational design
    God as math geek and, 124
religious services
    farting encouraged during, 58
    Marvel films as, 131
rights
    absence of God-given, 68–70
"Rise and Shine (The Noah
        Song)," 24
Roosevelt, Franklin D., 113
Roosevelt, Theodore, 112

saints
    large number of obscure, 53
    rarified type, 53
    usual fate of, 16
Sanders, Bernie
    God voted for, 72
saving
    God overloaded with requests
        for, 36
    the queen or king, 74
Second Amendment
    Constitution as referring solely
        to, 82
    passionate defense of, 68
Second Coming
    knocketh knocketh jokes on,
        109–10
    See also end times
Second Dumbing, 8

self-fruitful non-multiplying. See
        masturbation
Sentinelese people, 26–28
Sermon on the Mount
    Jesus mentions "douchebag"
        in, 57
Seventh-day Adventist Church,
        200
sexism
    God assembles panel on, 159–61
sexual innuendo
    blessings and, 141
    Holy Ghost's habits and, 9
    Matthew 14:29 and, 8
    Pslam 69 and, 142
sexuality
    cleaning up after, 143
    masturbation, 143–44, 145–46
    See also sexual innuendo
Shakespeare, William, 111
shanda for the goyim, 50
sheep
    as socialism metaphor, 71–72
Shelley, Percy Bysshe, 87
shopping
    Christmas, 166–67
    COVID and, 138
    online, 11
shrug emoticon, 21–23
Simon. See Peter
Sinetar, Marsha, 113
skin-care products
    approved by God, 140
slavery
    Jefferson's hypocrisy and, 70
sneezes
    blessings not available for, 141

Ugaritic pejoratives, 64–65
ultraviolet range of moral
    spectrum, 53

vaccines
    desperate waiting for, 138
veganism
    as Earth-friendly, 153
viruses
    as equal children of God,
    140

wealth distribution
    God still waiting for, 37–38
    as sheep shearing, 72
Weinstein, Harvey, 50
What Would Jesus Do? (WWJD),
    21–23

white people
    whining by, 162–63
white privilege
    constitutional amendment
        banning reference to, 82
Whitman, Walt, 111
who's the best?, 134–35
Wilde, Oscar, 112
wildfires
    as metaphor, 122
    who can tame?, 187–88
Wonder, Stevie, 79
Wordsworth, William, 62
"Wreck of the *Edmund Fitzgerald,*
    The," 172

Zeus
    guest acrostic by, 93–94

About the Author

GOD is a circle whose center is everywhere and whose circumference is nowhere, a comedian playing for an audience too afraid to laugh, and a concept by which we measure our pain. His previous works (all done in mysterious ways) include playing dice with the universe, shutting doors while opening windows, making little green apples, only knowing, blessing, damning, forsaking, forbidding, forgiving, willing, providing, speeding, soul-resting, Queen-saving, helping those who help themselves, and never giving anyone more than they can handle. He lives in His heaven, His own country, His green earth, and His little acre with His wife Mary and his children Zach, Jesus, and Kathy. If he did not exist, it would be necessary to invent him.

David Javerbaum is the 13-time Emmy-winning comedy writer behind the parody Twitter account @TheTweetOfGod, which has more than 6.2 million followers and inspired the hit Broadway play *An Act of God*. He was the longtime head writer and executive producer of *The Daily Show with Jon Stewart* and the coauthor of that show's bestsellers *America (The Book)* and *Earth (The Book)*. He is also a Grammy-winning and Tony-nominated lyricist.